THE STRUCTURED LITERACY PLAYBOOK

Preplanned Lessons for Building Phonics and Fluency Skills

MELISSA ORKIN, SARAH GANNON, AND ALEXANDRIA OSBURN

FOREWORD BY MARYANNE WOLF

 DK Learning

Produced for DK by
BookLife Publishing
OMNI House, King's Lynn, Norfolk PE30 4LS

Authors
Melissa Orkin, Ph.D.
Sarah Gannon, M.Ed.
Alexandria Osburn, M.S.Ed.

Senior Editor Amelia Jones
Project Art Editor Anna Scully
Managing Editor Katherine Neep
Managing Art Editor Sarah Corcoran
Senior Production Editor Andy Hilliard
Senior Production Controller Meskerem Berhane
Publisher Sarah Forbes
Managing Director, Learning Hilary Fine

First American Edition, 2025
Published in the United States by DK Publishing,
a division of Penguin Random House LLC
1745 Broadway, 20th Floor, New York, NY 10019

Published in Great Britain by Dorling Kindersley Limited

ISBN: 978-0-5939-7094-2

DK books are available at special discounts when purchased in bulk for sales promotions, premiums, fund-raising, or educational use.
For details, contact: DK Publishing Special Markets,
1745 Broadway, 20th Floor, New York, NY 10019
SpecialSales@dk.com

Printed and bound in China

www.dk.com

This book was made with Forest Stewardship Council™ certified paper – one small step in DK's commitment to a sustainable future.
Learn more at www.dk.com/uk/ information/sustainability

Contents

Foreword by Maryanne Wolf

In the ever-evolving field of literacy education, there is one shared goal among teachers, regardless of their particular method of teaching: that is, to enable every child to read and to understand that learning to read will give each of them a whole new world, a world where they can become their best selves. The authors of this book integrate the best of our field's theoretical knowledge and their many years of teaching experience to help every teacher teach every child. That said, there is an ongoing challenge faced by teachers today. How do they effectively meet the diverse needs of young learners, all the while adhering to evidence-based practices?

The Structured Literacy Playbook rises to this challenge, offering educators a practical and transformative approach to elementary literacy intervention. This book provides more than just guidance; it delivers a comprehensive framework for planning and delivering targeted instruction. By integrating pre-planned lessons aligned with the phases of word reading development, *The Structured Literacy Playbook* equips teachers with tools that bridge the gap between research and classroom practice. Each lesson goes beyond the surface of phonics instruction, embedding word reading strategies into meaningful literacy experiences that foster fluency, vocabulary growth, and comprehension. My own work on the new RAVE-O intervention program is based on what we have called the POSSUM approach. POSSUM is an acronym that stands for Phonology (sounds), Orthography (spelling), Semantics (vocabulary and its connections), Syntax (grammar), Understanding (comprehension), and Morphology (morphemes), and highlights a multi-component approach that develops, integrates, and automatizes knowledge across multiple aspects of word knowledge (Orkin et al, 2022; Wolf & Katzir-Cohen, 2001).

Principles from this work are incorporated in this book's wonderful ways of emphasizing the multiple components that go beyond phonics and that contribute to fluency and deep reading. One of the greatest gifts in the teaching profession is to watch how what we teach becomes part of the next generation's contributions. Dr. Melissa Orkin, one of the authors of this book, did her Ph.D. with me and continues to conduct work with me, particularly on fluency. I could not be prouder of what she has achieved and of what she and her co-authors have done in this book that will reach far more teachers than I ever could.

Designed specifically with educators in mind, the structure of *The Structured Literacy Playbook* reflects a deep understanding of classroom realities. Organized by increasingly complex phonics concepts, its chapters progress methodically, ensuring that each new strategy builds on previous knowledge. From continuous blending techniques for early readers in Chapter 1 to exploring multiple-meaning words in later chapters, the content evolves alongside students' developmental needs.

What sets *The Structured Literacy Playbook* apart is its seamless integration of foundational literacy elements with engaging, decodable texts from Phonic Books. Through a teacher-friendly format, it pairs clear, concise rationales for instructional routines with vibrant, well-illustrated examples. The inclusion of a link to access supplemental lesson materials ensures that educators have the resources they need at their fingertips.

At its core, *The Structured Literacy Playbook* recognizes that literacy is not just about decoding words, but also about understanding and using the multiple aspects of language effectively. Each lesson addresses a cohesive set of skills—phonics, sight word recognition, vocabulary, morphology, fluency, comprehension, and spelling—offering a holistic approach that supports oral and written language development.

Whether you are a seasoned educator looking to refine your practice or a newcomer seeking a structured path to literacy instruction, *The Structured Literacy Playbook* provides the insight, strategies, and resources to empower your teaching. It is more than a book—it is a guide to unlocking the potential of every young reader, one word at a time.

Maryanne Wolf is the Director of the Center for Dyslexia, Diverse Learners, and Social Justice at UCLA and has authored over 170 scientific publications and books, including Proust and the Squid: The Story, Tales of Literacy for the 21st Century, *and* Reader, Come Home. *She is co-author of the RAN/RAS naming speed tests and the creator of the RAVE-O Intervention Program for all striving readers.*

A proud teacher, Maryanne Wolf (left), and her doctoral student, Melissa Orkin (right). (2013)

Introduction

The Structured Literacy Playbook offers instructional strategies and lesson frameworks for practical, sequential, and efficient literacy development. Just as athletes require a balance of clear instruction and meaningful drills, students require support in developing their literacy skills. This book provides resources for educators to support skill development through thoughtful modeling, practice, and coaching. Each chapter focuses on a **Game Plan**, a Structured Literacy routine that functions as a model lesson, which is designed to accompany a decodable text. The high-leverage instructional routines that comprise each Game Plan are referred to as **Winning Strategies** due to the empirical evidence that supports their efficacy. Game Plans can be delivered to a variety of students in both small group and tutorial formats and can be modified to fit different practice schedules. **Example Practice Schedules** feature pacing guides for lesson delivery and take into consideration the requirements for skill consolidation and incremental learning.

While there are other established intervention approaches that may support teaching certain key literacy skills and strategies at different points, the multi-componential approach described in this book aligns with current literacy research. Regardless of the scope and sequence used for phonics instruction, the evidence-based strategies highlighted in this text were selected to enhance the resources and educational strategies used by all literacy educators.

Support for Educators

One of the most rewarding experiences as an elementary educator is building literacy skills in young students. Elementary teachers assert that literacy is fundamental for all other academic achievement (Hudson et al, 2021), yet ensuring grade-level performance among the majority of students remains a challenge for most educators. Over the last three decades, fourth grade reading proficiency rates have remained largely flat, with a significant decrease following the educational disruptions associated with COVID-19 (Di Pietro, 2023). In 2023, 37 percent of fourth graders in the US performed below a basic level of reading proficiency, which implies students are unable to reference, summarize, develop connections, and/or analyze text in a meaningful way (NAEP, 2023). Persistent low rates of reading proficiency have frustrated educators, families, researchers, and policymakers, as significant evidence suggests that when high-leverage systems and practices are in place, "reading failure can be prevented in all but a small percentage of children with serious learning disorders" (Moats, 2020).

Settled Science of Reading Instruction

The "settled" Science of Reading instruction asserts five major tenets:

1) Reading is unnatural (Wolf, 2007).

2) All children need some degree of explicit classroom instruction in fundamental literacy skills (phonemic awareness, phonics, fluency, vocabulary, and comprehension) (National Reading Panel (US), 2000).

3) Students who demonstrate risk for reading impairment require additional targeted instruction through small group intervention or tutoring (Gersten et al, 2020; Wanzek et al, 2018).

4) Literacy instruction that maximizes "explicit" pedagogical principles results in higher engagement and greater skill development (Archer & Hughes, 2011).

5) Targeted interventions that follow a Structured Literacy approach and integrate instruction on multiple aspects of word knowledge (i.e. phonics, vocabulary, morphology, syntax, and comprehension) result in significant gains in reading achievement (Donegan & Wanzek, 2021; Lovett et al, 2014; Morris et al, 2012).

Creating Practical Resources

This book has been developed to address the challenges that teachers experience. Our observations of literacy instruction span multiple decades and various locations in public schools, private schools, clinical settings, and research settings. Collectively, we have served as literacy coaches, classroom teachers, researchers, and clinical directors and, regardless of our position, we have witnessed dedicated, well-intentioned, bright teachers struggle to achieve their literacy goals because of the complexity of reading development. This book's Game Plans were developed to reduce the demands on teachers and employ high-leverage practices that support students as they embark into lifelong learning. Game Plans can be used by a wide range of practitioners, including general educators, specialists, paraprofessionals, and tutors.

Structured Literacy Instruction

One of the most promising findings in recent years has been the documented efficacy of Structured Literacy routines in efficiently developing foundational accuracy, fluency, and comprehension skills (Fletcher et al, 2018; Foorman et al, 2016; National Reading Panel (US), 2000). Structured Literacy is an instructional approach characterized by teaching that is explicit, systematic, and incremental, and integrates multiple aspects of word knowledge. Each pedagogical element of Structured Literacy has a strong body of empirical support that is often referred to as the Science of Reading.

Explicit instruction is considered a primary tool for ensuring equity among all students (Archer & Hughes, 2011). Teachers who use an explicit approach do not make assumptions about students' existing knowledge and provide clear models, offer plentiful opportunities for practice, and deliver immediate corrective feedback to ensure efficient learning. Explicit instruction features a high level of student engagement through streamlined teacher language and embedded strategies. These strategies are designed to maximize whole group participation and include choral responses and paired conversations.

Systematic and Incremental Instruction

Systematic and incremental instruction ensures that skills are taught in a meaningful sequence that progresses from simple to complex. An incremental approach introduces skills individually, and lessons are crafted to include continual review, which builds skills in a cumulative manner.

Teaching Multiple Aspects of Word Knowledge

Integrating multiple aspects of word knowledge into a Structured Literacy routine implies delivering instruction that connects phonemic awareness and phonics strategies to other aspects of linguistic information, such as vocabulary, parts of speech, and morphology. Literacy instruction that is multi-componential results in greater achievements than instruction that focuses on a single component (for example, phonemic awareness in isolation) (Donegan & Wanzek, 2021). There are several specialized, evidence-based intervention programs that have demonstrated effective outcomes teaching students all aspects of word knowledge (Lovett et al, 2014; Morris et al, 2012). Notable among them is the RAVE-O program (Wolf, 2011) originally developed by Maryanne Wolf and colleagues at the Tufts University Center for Reading and Language Research as a multi-componential approach for supporting reading fluency and comprehension at the elementary level. The RAVE-O program influenced both the lesson frameworks and instructional routines embedded in this book's Game Plans. The curriculum and its documented efficacy inspired our instructional choices for small group intervention. Of particular note, the curriculum emphasizes the importance of simultaneous instruction in efficient word recognition strategies, vocabulary development, and activities that build knowledge about parts of speech and morphology.

Evidence-Based Theories That Emphasize the Multiple Aspects of Word Knowledge

The power of multi-componential instruction lies in the coordinated activation of all language areas involved in the reading process. Nearly all of the most widely supported theories of reading development acknowledge the integrated nature of both word reading and language comprehension. These include the Simple View of Reading, which places equal importance on the contributions of decoding and language comprehension in reading comprehension (Gough & Tunmer, 1986), and the Reading Rope (Scarborough, 2001), which posits reading achievement as the result of language and decoding skills that become progressively more intertwined as students develop literacy abilities. Finally, the Four-Part Processing Model (Seidenberg & McClelland, 1989) is also rooted in the connectivist approach. It describes the interactive nature of multiple aspects of language knowledge, including phonological (sounds), orthographic (letter patterns), semantic (word meaning), and context in reading development.

Cognitive Evidence That Emphasizes the Multiple Aspects of Word Knowledge

Our neurological understanding of reading development strengthens and expands earlier theoretical models. Nicknamed "the Reading Circuit," neuroscientists have identified groups of working neurons that become deeply interconnected as reading skills develop (Dehaene, 2010; Wolf, 2017).

Unlike innate abilities, such as language processing, reading is not hardwired into the brain; it must be learned and constructed by repurposing existing neural systems for vision, language, and cognition. This reading circuit involves areas responsible for decoding letters and sounds (phonology), recognizing common letter patterns (orthography), activating word meanings (semantics), understanding parts of speech (syntax), and deciphering the ways in which morphemes (prefixes, suffixes, and roots) impact pronunciation and meaning (Wolf, 2017). To build fluency, it is critically important to develop automaticity (the ability to effortlessly read words without having to decode them) within and across each cognitive aspect of word knowledge (Benjamin & Gaab, 2012; Wolf & Katzir-Cohen, 2001).

The Role of Phonics Skills

Phonics has been well established as a critical element in reading instruction (National Reading Panel (US), 2000). Phonics describes the system by which sounds are represented by letters and letter patterns in writing. The English language largely follows rules about when to use different letter patterns to spell English sounds. Approximately 50 percent of English words follow these rules, and an additional 37 percent of words contain only one sound-based exception. In order to read and spell proficiently, it is necessary for students to learn the phonics rules and practice their direct application (National Reading Panel (US), 2000). The purpose of phonics skills is to develop automatic word recognition, in which students can automatically and instantaneously retrieve most words. Automatic word retrieval is a significant contributor to overall reading fluency and comprehension. This skill emerges in phases that are facilitated by explicit, systematic instruction, as described in the following section.

Developing Word Recognition Skills

There are several predictable phases of word recognition, originally theorized by Linnea Ehri (1995), which describe how children progress from non-readers to readers with automatic word recognition. This book's chapters are organized in a sequence that complements students' development of word recognition skills, beginning with the Partial Alphabetic Phase. The chapters in the book are designed to mirror the sequence of word recognition development while simultaneously featuring high-utility phonics skills.

Phase 1—Pre-Alphabetic: Students have not learned the phonic code and "read" words by visual cues and memorization. Most "reading" occurs with common logos or environment print (print that is seen in everyday life such as street signs). For example, words such as "open," "exit," and "stop."

Phase 2—Partial Alphabetic/Letters and Sounds: Students learn to decipher and manipulate the sounds in language, including matching letters to their corresponding sounds. In order to become proficient in the alphabetic principle, even for a handful of letters, students require instruction in complementary activities such as phonemic awareness tasks, knowledge of letter names, knowledge of letter sounds, and letter formation. However, knowledge of letter sounds in isolation is limited and, in order to read, students must move to the next skill involved in word recognition—decoding.

Phase 3—Full Alphabetic/Decoding: In the decoding phase of word recognition, students use their emerging knowledge of letter-sound correspondences to "sound out," or decode, words. A key skill in this phase involves the ability to maintain the accurate sequence of sounds while blending them together to pronounce a word—for example, the ability to accurately sequence the sounds /s/ /t/ /u/ /n/ /t/ and to correctly pronounce the word "stunt" instead of saying "stun" or "nuts." It is important to note that students do not need to know all the vowel sounds before they move to blending sounds together. Decoding can begin with one vowel sound and a handful of common consonants.

Phase 3.5—Partial Mapping: This additional phase is not part of Ehri's original theory; however, conceptualizing a midpoint from decoding to orthographic mapping can be helpful for instructional planning. The jump from decoding words to recognizing them instantaneously can be quite challenging for many students. Incorporating techniques that support partial mapping of words is useful for moving students away from the labor-intensive sound-by-sound reading and toward more efficient word recognition. By teaching students to recognize larger units or word parts, such as the rime pattern in a word (e.g. f<u>it</u>, d<u>ot</u>, cl<u>ap</u>, h<u>eld</u>, r<u>ipe</u>, sc<u>orn</u>, b<u>east</u>), educators support greater efficiency in reading as students move to sight word recognition (Kilpatrick, 2020).

Reading by Rime Pattern

Reading words by rime pattern involves directing students to pronounce the rime pattern before pronouncing the entire word. Although it seems counterintuitive to read starting with the middle letters in a word, decoding by rime pattern offers several advantages. The first advantage is that the rime pattern stabilizes the pronunciation of the vowel. Consider the ways in which the letter 'o' is pronounced in the following words: "go," "got," and "gown." The vowel pronunciation varies because the rime pattern indicates the word's syllable type. See Chapter 5 (pages 119–120) for more about the syllable type categories. The word "go" is an open syllable, and the vowel 'o' makes a long sound. The word "got" is a closed syllable, and the vowel 'o' makes a short sound. Finally, the word "gown" is a vowel diphthong, and the vowel 'o' combines with the letter 'w' to make a new vowel sound.

The pronunciation of the rime pattern activates a critical cue in our auditory memory for words. There is evidence to suggest that words are stored in our auditory memory by both initial sound and rime pattern and that it is more difficult to retrieve a word when activating our memory for the vowel sound in isolation (Kilpatrick, 2020).

Phase 4—Consolidated Alphabetic/ Orthographic Mapping: Word recognition development concludes with the ability to automatically pronounce the entire word without the need for decoding. The cognitive process that underlies our sight word knowledge is called orthographic mapping. Once a word has been mapped, it functions as an "old friend" and is instantly recognizable across texts.

Defining Sight Words and Heart Words

Sight words are any words that are recognized and read automatically, meaning that they do not need to be sounded out, or decoded. (Sight words vary from student to student, depending on which words have been mapped for automatic recognition.) Most sight words are also considered high-frequency words. That is to say that they are commonly occurring in text (e.g. people, the, of, because). Many high-frequency words follow regular phonics spelling patterns, but some might be irregularly spelled.

Heart words are high-frequency words that contain one or more irregular spelling patterns (e.g. said, was, from, there). The heart word approach emphasizes the use of traditional sound-spelling relationships and denotes any irregular spelling patterns with the symbol of a heart. When a word with advanced phonics patterns is introduced to younger students, we often discuss the notion of a "temporary heart word," meaning spelling patterns may seem irregular, but in later lessons students will learn the phonetic rule. For example, students in kindergarten will likely need to read and spell the word "like." While "like" is a phonetically regular word that follows the vowel-consonant-e pattern, most commercial phonics programs do not introduce this pattern until first grade. Educators can follow the same protocol for teaching both temporary and permanent heart words.

The Cycle of Word Recognition

The phases of word recognition are not finite, but iterative. Early in their reading career, students learn short vowel sounds and most consonants, then move through the phases of word recognition for short vowel words. As a broader range of phonics rules are introduced, students begin again with Phase 2 of word recognition. The speed at which students move through the phases is typically faster once they have mapped short vowel sounds or closed syllable words.

Integrating Vocabulary, Syntax, and Comprehension

Key areas of the reading circuit that are often overlooked during interventions include vocabulary, syntax, and comprehension processes. Developing vocabulary knowledge includes not only increasing the number of words students know, but also strengthening the depth of knowledge they possess about each word, known as their "semantic neighborhood" (Buchanan et al, 1996). Words with more associations live in a larger neighborhood. The size of a semantic neighborhood is positively associated with word recognition, with larger neighborhoods facilitating faster word recognition (Pexman et al, 2002). Successful vocabulary instruction not only introduces students to new words but also supports the development of robust associations. Teachers can employ active processing strategies that connect word meaning to students' experiences through questioning techniques, use of visual supports, and expanded dialogues (Beck et al, 2013).

Syntax refers to the system used to combine words in meaningful ways to create phrases and sentences. Knowledge of syntax includes parts of speech, grammar, and punctuation. Although syntax is often associated with writing instruction, syntactic skills also support reading fluency and comprehension. The ability to identify key phrases in a sentence (e.g. subject, predicate, and prepositional phrases) helps with automaticity, pacing, and expression. Additionally, syntactic processes bridge word recognition to comprehension.

The ultimate goal of word recognition instruction is to facilitate fluent comprehension of texts. Although decodable texts are limited in their use of varied and complex language, opportunities to monitor comprehension are still available. Game Plan activities such as vocabulary instruction, sentence reading, and morphology practice all reinforce comprehension at the single word and sentence level. Story-level comprehension is supported through questions that address students' understanding of lexical knowledge (the meaning of words in text), factual knowledge (the ability to retrieve information), and inferential analysis (connecting clues from the text with background knowledge to understand and reason).

The Backward Planning Approach

Each Game Plan not only relies on a Structured Literacy framework but was also developed utilizing a backward planning approach. In backward planning, the lesson is developed from a decodable book in order to target specific phonics skills. Educators might select the book based on the scope and sequence of skill building used by their classroom curriculum, or they may use a diagnostic tool to identify areas that require remediation in small group or Tier 2 instruction. Backward planning involves excerpting sentences and single words for reading, spelling, and vocabulary practice. At times, additional words that provide practice with the targeted skills are supplemented to the lesson. Each chapter provides a roadmap titled **Planning for Game Day** which offers a sequence of steps to backward plan the type of lesson being modeled.

Chapter Scope and Sequence

Chapter 1: Beginning Decoding aligns with the Partial Alphabetic Phase and features instruction that supports blending sounds. Typically considered a mid- to late-kindergarten skill, blending sounds accurately while reading is critical for early word recognition. Chapter 2: Developing Automaticity with Simple Decoding moves students beyond the continuous blending of individual sounds by introducing rime pattern instruction. This phase of word recognition is referred to as Partial Mapping and is characterized by the ability to recognize "chunks" of letters, such as the rime pattern.

The next two chapters support students' automatic word recognition as they encounter longer words. In Chapter 3: Early Sight Word Development, instruction guides students in efficiently recognizing words that include final consonant blends. Chapter 4: Building Stamina with Longer Words continues to enhance recognition skills with words that begin with consonant blends or digraphs. Chapter 5: Decoding Multisyllabic Words introduces students to strategies for dividing and efficiently decoding multisyllabic words with closed vowel sounds. Although educators often lament the significant proportion of time allocated to short vowel phonics patterns in early grades, it is important to keep in mind the utility of this knowledge. Short vowel patterns are the most common of all syllable types in English and provide students with strategies to decode approximately 40 percent of all words in the language (Stanback, 1992).

Although spelling activities are integrated into every chapter, Chapter 6: Spelling Strategies with Suffixes pays special attention to the connection between decoding and encoding. The chapter offers instructional strategies for teaching spelling generalizations when adding suffixes. Spelling with suffixes is a common challenge in elementary school and can bottleneck fluency with written expression.

Chapter 7: Decoding New Vowel Sounds, the final chapter, features instruction on automatic word recognition with long vowel words that contain a final silent 'e' (e.g. vowel-consonant-e or VCe). Once students have orthographically mapped the two most common syllable types (closed and VCe), they should be able to command approximately 50 percent of English words (Stanback, 1992).

Scope and Sequence of
The Structured Literacy Playbook

Chapters	Phonics Concept	Example Words	Additional Aspects of Word Knowledge
Chapter 1: Beginning Decoding	Continuous Blending of Single-Syllable Two- and Three-Letter Short Vowel Words (VC and CVC)	it, sit, at, sat	Integration of Vocabulary Instruction
Chapter 2: Developing Automaticity with Simple Decoding	Rime Pattern Recognition of Two- and Three-Letter Short Vowel Words (VC and CVC)	map, cap, sad, mad	Irregular Word/Heart Word Instruction
Chapter 3: Early Sight Word Development	Rime Pattern Recognition of Four-Letter Short Vowel Words with Final Consonant Blends (CVCC)	bunk, junk, best, rest	Use of RAN Charts Developing Associations to Vocabulary Words
Chapter 4: Building Stamina with Longer Words	Recognition of Four- and Five-Letter Short Vowel Words with Initial Consonant Blends or Digraphs (CCVC and CCVCC); Suffix –s	trust, crust	Exploring Multiple-Meaning Word Vocabulary
Chapter 5: Decoding Multisyllabic Words	Reading and Spelling Multisyllabic Words with Short Vowel Syllables; Syllable Division; Suffix –s/–es	sandpit, muffin	Practicing Spelling Rules for Suffix –s and –es
Chapter 6: Spelling Strategies with Suffixes	Spelling Strategies for Single- and Multi-Syllable Short Vowel Words with Suffixes –ed and –ing	scanned, grabbed, mittens	Understanding the Purpose of Common Suffixes Exploring Parts of Speech and Phrasing in Sentences
Chapter 7: Decoding New Vowel Sounds	Rime Pattern Recognition of VCe Words with and without Consonant Blends	slime, crime, stone	Spelling Rules for VCe Words

Pairing Lessons with Decodable Texts

Decodable texts are most productive when learned phonics patterns align closely with the words in a text (Lindsey, 2022). Furthermore, when students are able to reliably apply decoding skills, they rely less on compensatory reading strategies (e.g. context clues, pictures). These strategies are commonly used by weak readers who lack strong word recognition skills (Stanovich et al, 1986; Tunmer & Chapman, 2012). Structured Literacy intervention is more effective when students are able to apply word reading skills directly to texts (Spear-Swerling, 2024).

Recommendations for Structure and Duration of Intervention

Recent meta-analyses of supplemental interventions found that students who are placed in small groups of similarly skilled students and receive 20–40 minutes at least three times a week make the most effective progress (Gersten et al, 2008). The flexibility of the Game Plans allow various schedules and intervention formats. Suggested practice schedules accompany each chapter to maximize skill consolidation and efficient learning. Just as an athlete develops skills in a sequential manner, the chapters in this book enhance young readers' skill development by initially teaching skills, then offering practice through drills to develop mastery, automaticity, and stamina. The application to text allows readers to generalize their skills in the way that players exhibit their talents in competition.

Text Types and Purposes

Decodable texts are characterized by the level of control exerted on the variety of phonics patterns, irregular words, and specialized vocabulary in the book. Texts are considered decodable when at least 64 percent of the words can be sounded out using phonics rules (but this can extend to 95 percent) (Reading Rockets, 2024). Strong decodable texts serve as a platform for practicing word recognition and demonstrating literacy integrity (e.g. comprehensible and engaging) (Anderson et al, 1985).

Authentic texts in early literacy instruction are created for real-world purposes rather than for teaching a specific word recognition skill (Duke et al, 2006). These texts are typically rich in natural language patterns that are a mix of decodable and non-decodable words. Authentic texts may be organized by Lexile or grade level.

For additional resources, please visit https://geni.us/structuredlitplaybook

Chapter 1
Beginning Decoding

- Utilizing continuous blending to jump-start initial VC and CVC word reading

- Introducing a multisensory approach to spelling instruction for VC and CVC words

Game Plan

Phonemic Awareness

it	sit	Tim
sat	Sam	Tam

Phonics Concept

Provide direct instruction in the phonics concept, utilizing words pulled from the Reader and/or that fit the patterns you are teaching.

Letter/Sound Review

s	a	t	i	m

Single Word Reading

it	sit	Tim	sat

Sentence Reading

"I am Tim."

It is Tam.

Tam sat.

Vocabulary

Which word finishes this sentence: I don't like ___? (it)	Which word refers to a character in the story? (Tim)	Which word is an action that occurred in the past? (sat)	Which word is the opposite of stand? (sit)

Story and Comprehension Questions

Who are the characters in the story?	What does Sam tell Tim to do?	Who is the last friend to sit?

Dictation

Say (repeat word)	sit			sat		
Move (segment word)	🔵	🟠	⚪	🔵	🔵	⚪
Spell (letter tiles)	s	i	t	s	a	t
Write (write word)	s	i	t	s	a	t

Target Skills for Game Plan

Early in reading development, students move through two phases of word recognition. These phases are critical to later reading fluency and comprehension.

During the Partial Alphabetic/Letters and Sounds Phase, students develop their understanding of the alphabetic principle—that sounds in English are represented by a letter or letters. Once letter-sound knowledge has been introduced, students move to the next phase of word recognition—decoding.

The Full Alphabetic/Decoding Phase of word recognition is characterized by movement from isolated letter-sound knowledge to blending letter sounds and pronouncing whole words. Instruction in this phase supports the development of students' ability to blend sounds in the correct sequence, starting with simple, two- and three-letter short vowel words (e.g. in, bat, hop). The Game Plan for this chapter has been developed to provide a framework for teachers to refer to when moving students into the Decoding Phase of reading. Along these lines, the activities and instruction provided in the Game Plan are designed to develop the following two skills in students who are just beginning to read:

- Decoding one-syllable two- and three-letter short vowel words (VC and CVC)
- Spelling one-syllable two- and three-letter short vowel words (VC and CVC)

Your Team

Students are ready for this Game Plan when they demonstrate knowledge of several consonants and at least one vowel sound. In order to jump-start decoding instruction, teachers can prioritize teaching their students strategies for blending as soon as a handful of consonant sounds and one short vowel sound have been introduced.

It is unnecessary to instruct students in all letter-sound correspondences before this critical skill can begin. Consider the requirements to blend simple VC and CVC words such as "at," "sat," "pat," and "sap." In order to accurately decode these words, students only need to know the letter-sound correspondences for the four letters, 's,' 'a,' 't,' and 'p.' Educators should refer to their phonics scope and sequence to identify at what point such instruction in this phase of word reading can begin.

Jump-Start Guide to Decoding

Scope Sample

Letters Taught	Sounds	Words to Blend
s, a, t, i, m	at am it	at, mat, sat am, Tam, Sam it, sit
n, o, p	ap at in ip it ot op	In addition to the words above: nap, tap, sap, map Nat, pat in, pin, tin nip, sip, tip, pip pit, sit tot, not, pot top, mop, pop

Scope Sample 2

Letters Taught	Sounds	Words to Blend
t, b, f, n, m, i, u	it ib if in im ut ub un	bit, fit bib, fib if tin, bin, fin Tim but, nut tub bun, fun, nun

Case Study

Cameron is a kindergartener who knows the names of the letters in her name. She is working to develop both accuracy and automaticity with additional sound-symbol (letter-sound) correspondences. During phonemic awareness and phonics instruction, her teacher notices her difficulty blending sounds into words. For example, when she attempts to blend /s/ /i/ /t/, she might say "tis." During small group instruction, her teacher reports that she identifies each sound in the word, but when attempting to pronounce the word as a unit, she is often inaccurate. What strategies can help Cameron become more accurate in both reading and spelling?

Training Camp

Before students are ready to blend sounds into words, they need to be accurate with a handful of consonants and at least one vowel. The following Training Camp exercises can lead to greater success in developing subsequent reading skills. These exercises incorporate multisensory techniques by including articulation cues during pronunciation to differentiate sounds of letters, as well as the use of letter formation strategies to consolidate sound-symbol correspondence knowledge.

Articulation

All letter sounds are produced through combined use of the lips, tongue, teeth, breath, and soft palate. These movements, along with the vibration of the vocal cords, or lack thereof, work in a unique way to produce the nuanced sounds in the English language. In order to read, students must connect letters to their articulated sounds.

The /b/ sound is produced by closing the lips in a tight straight line, then building up pressure and quickly releasing in a lip-popping movement. Some programs refer to this letter as a lip-popper or stop consonant. There are two lip-popper sounds in English—one that is voiced (/b/), and one that is unvoiced (/p/).

Voiced sounds are those that are produced by vibrating vocal cords (for example, the sounds /m/, /r/, and /v/). Unvoiced sounds are produced without making a vocal cord vibration (for example, the sounds /s/, /t/, /f/). Grouping consonant letters by their voiced and unvoiced pairs is an efficient way to cluster sounds for students and support the activation of multisensory cues during articulation.

Letter Formation

In order to help students associate the articulation of a letter's sound with the visual formation of the letter, educators can connect letter-sound instruction with handwriting. Handwriting involves motor planning and sequencing skills, similar to the skills required for the clear articulation of letter sounds. Research suggests that pairing formation practice with three utterances—naming the letter, naming the keyword, and naming the sound—can help to solidify this knowledge in the visual word form area of the brain (McCandliss et al, 2003). In practice, students might name the letter, keyword, and sound as they produce the three strokes involved in forming the letter. For the letter 'd,' students write the straight line while saying the letter name "d." As they trace the line back up midway, they would say the keyword ("dog," for example). Finally, as they complete the half-circle belly of the letter, they say /d/. For letters with only one or two letter strokes, prompt students to begin their utterances as they put pencil to paper. The connection between the three utterances and strokes can support students in solidifying their letter-sound knowledge.

Your Equipment

Series: Dandelion Launchers Extras Stages 1-7 (ISBN 9781783693450)

Reader: *I am Sam* (Book 1a)

Phonics Concept:

Continuous blending of one-syllable two- and three-letter short vowel words (VC and CVC).

Book Overview:

Two friends play in a park and hijinks ensue on the seesaw.

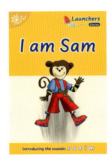

Text from the Book *I am Sam*

"I am Sam."

"I am Tim."

"Sit, Tim."

It is Tam.

Tam sat.

"Tim!"

Additional Texts

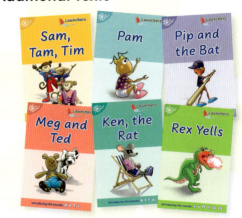

The **Dandelion Launchers Stages 1-7** (ISBN 9781783692835) and **Dandelion World Stages 1-7** (ISBN 9780744095609) series follow the same scope and sequence as the **Dandelion Launchers Extras Stages 1-7**, thereby providing the opportunity for instruction and application in additional texts before moving on to the next set of letter-sound correspondences.

Planning for Game Day

Game Plans are designed to provide a framework for the application of targeted phonics skills. In order to fully align practice of skills with application to connected text, we recommend utilizing a backward planning approach. First, select the instructional focus area and a decodable text that will help reinforce the development of the targeted skills. From there, identify three sentences containing words with the target skill. These words will be used for phonemic awareness instruction, single word reading, dictation, and vocabulary. For the Letter/Sound Review, identify sounds that students need to blend together for single word reading. Finally, set a purpose for reading and craft a variety of questions that support reading comprehension. The sequence for backward planning is shared in the following breakout box on page 22.

Backward Planning Using a Decodable Text

Planning Reading Activities (Sentences, Single Words, and Letter Sounds)

Step 1: Choose three sentences from the text. Select sentences that offer practice for target phonics skills.

Step 2: Select four individual words that appear in the sentences for single word reading practice.

Step 3: Choose the letters and rime patterns from the single word practice to teach sound-symbol correspondence.

Planning Phonemic Awareness Activity

Use the words from the single word reading activity for phonemic awareness (blending).

Planning Dictation Activity

Choose two words for the Move It, Spell It, Write It activity.

Planning Vocabulary and Comprehension Activities

Step 1: Develop questions that inquire about the meanings of the single words previously practiced.

Step 2: Read the text and craft questions that require students to find the information in the text (factual questions) and set a purpose for reading by asking students to keep a particular question in mind as they read the book.

Winning Strategies

The instructional routines in the Game Plan support the ongoing development of students' word recognition skills through two Winning Strategies:

- Utilizing continuous blending to jump-start initial VC and CVC word reading
- Introducing a multisensory approach to spelling instruction for VC and CVC words

Utilizing Continuous Blending to Jump-Start Reading

Continuous blending is an evidence-based instructional strategy that enhances decoding accuracy in the early phases of reading development. Continuous blending is an alternative method to segmenting and re-coding sounds. Phonics instruction that introduces decoding using a sound-by-sound blending approach focuses on retrieval of individual letter sounds, followed by the integration of sounds to produce a word. For example, to decode the word "mat," students are taught to point or tap under the letter 'm' and say /m/, point to the letter 'a' and say /a/, point to the last letter and say /t/, and then blend the sounds to pronounce the word "mat." There are many children who struggle with the segmentation approach to decoding and have a tendency to blend the sounds incorrectly or add additional sounds. For those students, the challenge lies in their ability to hold the individual sounds in the correct order, which facilitates accurate decoding. In contrast, when instruction features continuous blending, students are taught to sound out the word without pausing between sounds. Research that compared continuous blending with segmented blending found that students who received brief instruction on continuous blending demonstrated increased accuracy when decoding nonsense words (Gonzalez-Frey & Ehri, 2021). This strategy is explored in greater detail in Step 2 (page 25).

Introducing a Multisensory Approach to Spelling Instruction

Students' phonemic awareness skills, their decoding ability, and their spelling knowledge each make an important independent contribution to word reading achievement. However, achievement is maximized when students are able to integrate their knowledge of the sound structure of language, letter-sound correspondences, and rules for spelling (Moats & Brady, 2000). In the Move It, Spell It, Write It activity (see pages 33–34 for more about this activity), students segment the target word into its sounds, match the sounds to the associated letter tile, and then write (spell) the word. The activity integrates development in key foundational areas. In this way, phonemic awareness, decoding, and encoding are able to reinforce spelling achievement and overall literacy growth.

Executing Your Game Plan

Step 1: Maximize Phonemic Awareness Instruction

Phonemic awareness is the ability to recognize, identify, and manipulate individual sounds, or phonemes, in spoken words. In order to engage in phonemic awareness activities, students must develop their auditory memory to distinguish between increasingly complex sequences of sounds. For example, in preschool, most students can only correctly sequence large units of orally presented sounds (e.g. bath-tub, pop-corn). However, by elementary school, a combination of explicit instruction and purposeful practice expands students' abilities to sequence individual units of sound (e.g. /s/, /u/, /n/). These skills build students' auditory memory, which serves as an important cognitive tool during decoding. As children decode, they must hold individual letter sounds in their auditory memory to accurately read a word. For some students, sequencing challenges begin at the auditory level and phonemic awareness instruction will target development of their auditory memory (National Reading Panel (US), 2000). The words chosen for the Game Plan include the targeted phonics skill. Some words are selected because students will read them in later activities. Other words support generalization of phonemic awareness abilities.

Words for Phonemic Awareness Blending Activity in Game Plan

Sounds to Blend	Whole Word
/i/ /t/	it
/s/ /i/ /t/	sit
/t/ /i/ /m/	Tim
/s/ /a/ /t/	sat
/s/ /a/ /m/	Sam
/t/ /a/ /m/	Tam

Sound-Blending Routines

As noted earlier, the phonemic awareness activity that precedes reading is always a blending activity because this offers appropriate practice for sequencing sounds in auditory memory. Critics of phonemic awareness cite the limitations of instruction in the sounds of language without connection to letters and text (Rehfeld et al, 2022). Therefore, educators should be cognizant of the pacing of instruction to ensure phonemic awareness activities do not exceed a few minutes. As students make errors, quick corrective feedback is recommended. Corrective feedback offers the accurate response and encourages students to reproduce the correct response in a "my turn" (teacher produces accurate response) and "your turn" (students produce accurate response) format.

Teacher Script for Introducing, Modeling, and Practicing Phonemic Awareness

Introduction to Strategy
Teacher: *We are going to play a mystery word game. I am going to give you the sounds, and you are going to blend them together to say the word.*

Type of Words
Choose words from the Single Word Reading section of the Game Plan or additional words that follow the same phonics concept.

Teacher Language and Prompt for Modeling
Teacher: *Watch me hold up a finger for each sound. When I connect my fingers, you will blend the sounds to say the mystery word.*

Hold up a finger as you say each sound.

Start with the pointer finger on your left hand if facing students.
    Teacher: */i/ /t/*
Connect your two fingers together.
    Teacher: *"it"*

Differentiating Instruction or Corrective Feedback

Students might incorrectly pronounce the word.

Teacher: *My turn.* (Repeat the sounds in the word, hold up a finger for each sound, and correctly pronounce the word.)

Teacher: *Your turn.* (Have the students hold up a finger while saying each sound in the word and, when they connect their fingers, pronounce the word correctly.)

Differentiation of Phonemic Awareness Instruction

Phonemic awareness is most effective when students are familiar with the meaning of the target word. If students are unfamiliar with the target word, it is recommended that educators offer an image of the word. For example, a picture of a character in a box (e.g. Tam) or less common vocabulary (e.g. picnic, cloth) could populate or be revealed once students have blended the sounds together.

Step 2: Teach Phonics Concepts Using Winning Strategy

The target skill for the first Game Plan is decoding VC and CVC words. To support students in developing decoding skills, the lesson incorporates continuous blending as a Winning Strategy. Model the continuous blending strategy with words the students will encounter during the Single Word Reading activity. Other words with the same target phonics skill may be incorporated for additional practice.

 WINNING STRATEGY: Continuous Blending

In continuous blending, or connected phonation, students are explicitly taught to sound out the word without stopping or pausing between sounds. When first modeling continuous blending, choose CVC words that begin with a continuous consonant sound (e.g. f, l, m, n, f, s, v, and z). These consonant sounds can be stretched out as far as your breath can sustain. Continuous sounds are easily connected to vowel sounds. It should be noted that all vowels are continuous as well. Therefore, using continuous blending for the word "mat" would sound like /mmmaaaaat/.

Teacher Script for Teaching Continuous Blending

Introduction to Strategy

Teacher: *We are going to practice a strategy today called continuous blending. When we continuously blend, we turn our voices on to blend through the entire word without turning our voices off.*

Type of Words

Two- or Three-Letter Closed Syllable Short Vowel Words (VC or CVC Words)

Teacher Language and Prompt for Modeling

Write "it" on the board.

Teacher: *Watch me. I will sweep my finger underneath each letter while saying the sound for that letter. I will hold the sound, or keep my voice on, and then glide into the sound for the next letter until I get to the last letter. This helps me blend all the sounds together without stopping. Then, I will repeat the word in a clear and crisp way.*

Sweep your finger underneath the word "it."

Teacher: */iiiiiiiit/. "it." Let's try it together. As I sweep my finger under the letters, you say and hold the sounds. I will quickly underline the word and you will repeat the word.*

For the word "sit," point to the letter 's.' Students should say /sssss/, holding the sound until your finger moves to the letter 'i.' They will add /i/ to /sssss/ so it sounds like /ssssiii/. As you sweep your finger under the 't,' students will add /t/ to /ssssiii/ and say /ssssiiit/—"sit."

Repeat for all single words and any additional applicable practice.

Teacher: *Now let's practice with a few more.*

Supporting Students Having Difficulty with Continuous Blending

When selecting words for continuous blending practice, educators can choose between words that begin with continuous consonants or stop consonants.

Consonants with Continuous Sounds
f, l, m, n, r, s, v, z

Consonants with Stop Sounds
b, c (hard c), d, g, k, p, t

Students who struggle with continuous blending need practice with words that begin with continuous consonants (e.g. sat, mat, sit). Continuous consonants allow the sound to be held for several seconds. Stop consonants are sounds that are made quickly because they are articulated by stopping air flow. Stop sounds are best reserved for the end of words if students are struggling to blend. If there is a stop sound at the beginning of a word, it is often best to quickly jump off the stop consonant and link it to the vowel (e.g. /tttttim/—"Tim").

Step 3: Reinforce Letters/Sounds in Isolation

In order to help students build accuracy and automaticity in matching a letter or letters to the corresponding sound(s), the Game Plan includes opportunities to practice identifying letters and sounds that appear in the text in isolation before reading them in words. The lesson features five individual letters ('s,' 'a,' 't,' 'i,' 'm').

In some phonics programs, 'am' is considered a glued, or welded, sound because the nasalized /m/ alters the pronunciation of the short vowel, making it difficult to hear the individual sounds when segmenting.

Letter/Sound Review for Game Plan

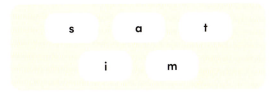

Supporting Students Having Difficulty with Sound-Symbol Correspondence

Letter sounds are most efficiently taught when students accurately demonstrate basic articulation and phonemic awareness skills. For students who are having difficulty, consider these modifications:

- Present consonant sounds with a "clipped" pronunciation and avoid the addition of a schwa, which can confuse students. For example, the clipped pronunciation of the letter 'b' is /b/, as opposed to /buh/, which adds a schwa.

- Provide additional opportunities for phonemic awareness instruction, where students practice breaking apart the sounds in language.

- Teach articulation cues for letter sounds by helping students feel the placement of their lips, teeth, and tongue.

- Integrate sound-symbol and handwriting instruction so that students are able to recognize the letter, pair the letter with the corresponding sound, and form the letter appropriately.

Teacher Script for Introducing, Modeling, and Practicing Letter/Sound Review

Introduction to Strategy

Teacher: *We are going to review some letters and sounds to help us with our reading.*

Type of Words

Choose individual consonants and vowels from the Game Plan.

Teacher Language and Prompt for Modeling

Write the first letter to review on a whiteboard or utilize letter-sound cards from your curriculum resources.

Teacher: *The letter is ___.* (Point to the letter and say the letter name.)

Students repeat.

Teacher: *The sound is _____.* (Point to the letter and say the sound.)

Students repeat.

Continue with each letter or pattern to complete the routine.

If using letter-sound cards from a different curriculum, include the keyword or image as necessary. Note that the keyword is used to support students in the appropriate production of the sound. It is important to fade this scaffold once students are able to accurately produce the sound.

Maintaining a "Perky Pace"

In order to keep the lesson moving at a "perky pace," it is important to establish a routine that maximizes students' engagement with the material. In the book *Explicit Instruction: Effective and Efficient Teaching*, Archer and Hughes emphasize the importance of whole group participation (Archer & Hughes, 2011). They recommend teaching students a signal (verbal and/or nonverbal) that cues choral responses. Just as a chorus includes the voices of all participants, choral responses invite all students to answer simultaneously. For example, you might tap your finger under the letter(s) and teach students to respond with the sound, or you might tap and say "sound" to elicit a quick, choral response from all students. Choral responses are a powerful interactive tool when there is one brief, correct answer. If students answer incorrectly, teachers can prompt corrective feedback in a "my turn, your turn" manner. Archer and Hughes recommend refraining from relying on individual turn-taking or hand-raising during these periods of instruction because doing so reduces opportunities for engagement and hampers the pace of instruction. When there is more than one correct answer, teachers can utilize a turn-and-talk method, in which students are paired and take turns sharing their ideas. (See Chapter 2 (page 56) for more about the turn-and-talk method.)

Step 4: Apply Phonics Concept to Single Words from the Text

The lesson's single words achieve three goals: they are in the story, they are in the sentences you have selected, and they provide the opportunity for students to practice the target phonics skill(s). The Game Plan features four words from the story *I am Sam* (e.g. it, sit, Tim, sat). See the **Teacher Script for Continuous Blending** on page 26 to practice continuous blending with single words from the text.

Individual Words for Game Plan

it   sit   Tim   sat

Step 5: Practice Reading Sentences from the Text

The sentence reading routine provides students with an opportunity to apply their decoding skills to connected text. Ideal sentences contain words with the target phonics concept and are comprehensible as standalone sentences. In some cases, it may be necessary to modify the sentence slightly to replace a pronoun with the name of the character. Students read these sentences prior to reading the decodable text, so it can be helpful to choose sentences that highlight characters' names and allude to important components or events in the text. For the Game Plan, we have selected the following sentences from *I am Sam* because they include a variety of VC and CVC words and introduce two of the characters in the story.

Sentences for Game Plan

"I am Tim."

It is Tam.

Tam sat.

Step 6: Expand Text-Related Vocabulary Knowledge

A key feature that distinguishes Structured Literacy instruction from solitary phonics instruction is the integration of various aspects of word knowledge. Vocabulary is a critical aspect of word knowledge, as it supports both reading fluency and comprehension. As students build beginning decoding skills, connections between word recognition abilities and comprehension occur partially through vocabulary instruction. In fact, a prominent theory of reading comprehension developed by Philip Gough and William Tunmer, called the Simple View of Reading, suggests that reading comprehension is the product of decoding skills and language comprehension skills, including vocabulary knowledge (Gough & Tunmer, 1986).

Evidence indicates that students recognize words not only because of their knowledge of letters and their corresponding sounds but also because of their knowledge of the word's meaning. Strong vocabulary knowledge allows readers to access a mental lexicon, a mental dictionary of words, which aids in fluent reading by helping them recognize and interpret words effortlessly (Perfetti, 2007). As readers grow their vocabulary, they develop a better understanding of these linguistic features, which makes it easier to recognize words even in varied contexts (Ehri, 2005). This connection is particularly crucial for young readers as they acquire foundational reading skills and become capable of reading fluently (National Reading Panel (US), 2000).

The Game Plan features a simple vocabulary activity where teachers review meanings for previously practiced individual words. Questions can incorporate references to synonyms, antonyms, and characters in the story, or they may offer students opportunities to complete a sentence. Prior to the activity, display the words from the Single Word Reading portion of the Game Plan. Have students chorally read the list before beginning to ask the questions.

Support Language Comprehension among Multilingual Learners

For students who are learning English as a new language, it might be helpful to provide images along with each of the single words for this activity. Linking the sounds, spelling, and meaning will help support students in developing both their word recognition and language comprehension skills.

Words and Questions for Vocabulary Activity

Game Plan: *I am Sam*	Questions
sat	Which word is an action that occurred in the past?
Tim	Which word refers to a character in the story?
it	Which word finishes this sentence? I don't like_____.
sit	Which word is the opposite of stand?

Game Plan: *On the Mat*	Questions
mat	Which word means a small rug?
sat	Which word completes the blank in this sentence? When I got home, I _____ down to eat.
Tim	Which word or words refer to a character in the story?
sit	Fill in the blank in this sentence. Before I give my dog a treat, I tell him to _____.

Step 7: Putting It All Together for Text Reading and Comprehension

The book reading portion of the Game Plan offers students the opportunity to apply their single word reading and sentence reading skills in connected text. Practicing connected text reading is a critical tool in helping improve students' accuracy, fluency, and comprehension (National Reading Panel (US), 2000). During this portion of the Game Plan, including a series of comprehension questions that connect word reading with meaning is recommended. When crafting questions to go along with the decodable book, ensure that the questions can be answered by reading the text and not by referencing the pictures. Typical questions can include a range of question types. These may include literal, inferential, and evaluative questions, as well as questions based on vocabulary knowledge. Prior to asking students to read connected text, teachers can orient students to the book by previewing the title and illustrations with them. Furthermore, setting a purpose for students to aim for when reading supports active comprehension monitoring (e.g. "As we read, I want you to figure out the problem that our main character, called _____, encounters in the book," or "Let's read the story to find out what happens to the character called _____.")

Comprehension Questions for Game Plan

Factual
What are the characters in the story?

Factual
What does Sam tell Tim to do?

Inferential
Who is the last friend to sit?

Text from the Book *I am Sam*

"I am Sam."

"I am Tim."

"Sit, Tim."

It is Tam.

Tam sat.

"Tim!"

Use Choral or Partner Reading Instead of Round Robin

There are many ways teachers can support student engagement during text reading. Strong engagement activities will maximize participation and ensure that all students receive an adequate proportion of time to build their reading skills. The three primary engagement techniques are choral reading, partner reading, and whisper reading to oneself. These techniques are often interchangeable. Some educators might have all students chorally read the first two pages of text and then pair off to partner read the remainder of the story. Other teachers might opt for some students to partner read while other individuals read to themselves or to a teacher. The "oral" part of reading can be accomplished at full volume or at a whisper; the key feature is that the student is articulating the words and receiving auditory feedback by hearing their voice as they read the text aloud. Whisper phones are particularly helpful tools for this purpose. The strategy that should be actively avoided or used with minimal frequency is the "round robin" approach, where each student in a group takes a turn reading a line of text while the others follow along. When students are only responsible for a minimal portion of the text, it not only restricts skill building but also limits their opportunities to build stamina (Kuhn, 2014).

Step 8: Applying Phonics Knowledge to Dictation

The reciprocal connection between reading and spelling in literacy achievement has been well established in literature (Moats & Brady, 2000). Both reading and spelling rely on students' knowledge of sounds and corresponding letters. Spelling is often more challenging for students because, although English has a limited number of sounds (approximately 44 sounds/phonemes, depending on region and curricular tool), there are many different letter patterns, or graphemes, for spelling each sound. For example, the /ae/ sound (also depicted as /ā/ or /A/) can be spelled 'a,' 'a-e,' 'ay,' 'ai,' 'ea,' 'eigh,' and 'ey.' Most students require a comprehensive approach to spelling that simultaneously integrates their knowledge of all contributing skills, including the sounds in language (phonemic awareness), the letter patterns, and correct sequencing of each sound (phonics).

This Game Plan features a multisensory instructional strategy called Move It, Spell It, Write It that supports the integration of phonemic awareness, phonics skills, and letter formation skills as students spell words (Blachman et al, 2000). Later chapters fade these scaffolds in order to expand students' spelling from sounds and individual words to complex sentence writing. If at any time your students struggle with spelling, scaffolds from Move It, Spell It, Write It can be re-integrated into the lesson to support skill development.

 WINNING STRATEGY: Introducing a Multisensory Approach to Spelling Instruction

Move It, Spell It, Write It is a multisensory spelling activity that combines phonemic awareness, sound-symbol correspondence, and handwriting to practice the targeted phonics concept. It is a modified version of a widely used activity called Say-It-and-Write-It (Blachman et al, 2000). An Elkonin Spelling Mat is used for this activity.

Elkonin Boxes

Elkonin boxes, also called phoneme frames or sound boxes, are tools that can be used as part of a method of teaching that aids in the development of phonemic awareness skills. Students can practice the Move It, Spell It, Write It activity with these boxes. To use Elkonin boxes, teachers draw a series of boxes on paper or a whiteboard, with one box representing each sound in the target word. Students listen and repeat the target word, then move a token into each box for each phoneme in the word. For example, for the word "sat," the teacher would draw three boxes, one box for each of the sounds in "sat."

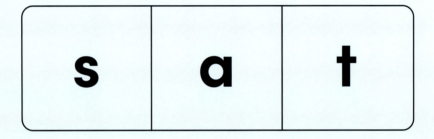

During the "Move It" portion of the activity, teachers provide students with an Elkonin Spelling Mat, present the word, and guide students in dividing the word into individual sound segments. Each sound is initially represented with a token, which students move into the appropriate Elkonin box. For some students, the initial target skill may involve simply completing the "Move It" portion of the exercise. Others are ready to progress to "Spell It."

During "Spell It," teachers guide students in identifying the letters that represent each sound in the Elkonin boxes. Then, they instruct them to place the appropriate letter tile or magnetic letter under the sound. Finally, in the "Write It" portion of the task, students write the letters to spell the target word. The Game Plan features two words—"sit" and "sat"—that follow the phonics concept and are featured in the Move It, Spell It, Write It activity.

Teacher Script for Delivering the Move It, Spell It, Write It Activity

Introduction to Strategy

Give students a Move It, Spell It, Write It paper, the appropriate number of tokens needed to represent each sound in the word, and letter tiles/magnetic letters that correspond to the letters in the target word in the Game Plan. Do not put the letters out in the correct sequence.

Teacher: *We are going to connect a word we have been reading to our spelling work.*

Teacher Language and Prompt for Move It

Teacher: *Today our word to spell is _____.*
Say _____.
Students repeat the word.
Teacher: *_____ has _____ sounds. Let's say each sound and move the tokens into the boxes below. Move one token for each sound you say.*

Students segment the word while simultaneously moving one token for each sound into an Elkonin box.

Teacher: *Say the word _____.*

Students complete the request.

Teacher Language and Prompt for Spell It

Teacher: *Now that we have identified the sounds in our word, let's use our letters to spell the sounds.*
Point to the first token in the Elkonin box, elicit the first sound, and have students match the sound with the correct letter tile/magnetic letter. Repeat for each token.

Teacher: *The sound ___ is spelled with the letter _____. (Elicit the letter name.)*
Repeat with each token until the word has been spelled with the letter tiles/magnetic letters.

Teacher Language and Prompt for Write It

If a specific handwriting or dictation paper is used in your phonics program, consider using it for this portion of the activity.
Teacher: *Now that we have spelled our word, let's write it. The word is ___.*
Students repeat the word.
Teacher: *The first sound in the word is ___. What letter do we write here?*
Students respond.

Teacher: *Write the letter _____.*
Model the letter formation on a whiteboard or paper, using language consistent with your handwriting instruction.
Repeat the procedure with each letter until students have written the word.
Teacher: *Let's read the word together.*
Students run a finger under the word while reading it.

Proposed Practice Schedule

The Game Plan in this chapter represents a set of eight instructional routines for small group instruction designed to be delivered over the course of several sessions. Research suggests that deliberate and spaced practice is effective for adopting new skills (Archer & Hughes, 2011). Although the practice schedule can be adjusted to align with your allotted instructional time, ensuring that there is dedicated time for connected text practice each day should be prioritized.

Day 1 (15 mins)	Day 2 (15 mins)
Phonemic Awareness (2 mins)	Vocabulary (3 mins)
Phonics Concept (4 mins)	Book Reading (5 mins)
Letter/Sound Review (2 mins)	Comprehension Questions (2 mins)
Single Words (2 mins)	Dictation (5 mins)
Sentences (5 mins)	

Game Plan

Decodable Text: *On the Mat*, Dandelion Launchers Extras Stages 1-7, Book 1b
Phonics Concept: **Continuous blending of one-syllable two- and three-letter short vowel words (VC and CVC)**

Phonemic Awareness

it	sat	mat
am	Sam	Tam

Phonics Concept

Provide direct instruction in the phonics concept, utilizing words pulled from the Reader and/or that fit the patterns you are teaching.

Letter/Sound Review

s	a	t	i	m

Single Word Reading

sat	mat	sit	Tim

Sentence Reading

I am Sam

It is Tim.

Tam sat.

Vocabulary

Which word means a small rug? (mat)	Which word completes the blank in this sentence? When I got home, I _____ down to eat. (sat)	Which word refers to a character in the story? (Tim)	Fill in the blank in this sentence. Before I give my dog a treat, I tell him to ___. (sit)

Story and Comprehension Questions

Who are the characters in the story?	What did Tam do?	Who sat first? Who sat last?

Dictation

Say (repeat word)	mat			Sam		
Move (segment word)	🟡	🔵	⚪	🔵	🔵	🟡
Spell (letter tiles)	m	a	t	s	a	m
Write (write word)	*m*	*a*	*t*	*S*	*a*	*m*

Chapter 2

Developing Automaticity with Simple Decoding

- Recognizing rime patterns in words

- Backward decoding

- Strategic instruction for heart words

- Reinforcing word recognition through spelling

Game Plan

Decodable Text: _Sit on It_, Dandelion Readers Set 3 Units 1–10, Book 1
Phonics Concept: Rime pattern recognition of two- and three-letter short vowel words (VC and CVC)

Phonemic Awareness

it	sit	Tim
at	sat	Tam

Phonics Concept

Provide direct instruction in the phonics concept, utilizing words pulled from the Reader and/or that fit the patterns you are teaching.

Letter/Sound/Rime Review

s	t	-at	-am	-it	-im

Single Word Reading

sit	sat	Sam	Tim

Heart Words

and

Sentence Reading

"Sam! Tam! Sit on it!"

Sam sat on it.

Tam, Tim, and Sam sat on it.

Vocabulary

Which words are names? (Sam/Tim/Tam)	Which word completes the blank in this sentence? I am tired and need to find a chair to ____ in? (sit)	Which word is the opposite of stand? (sit)	Which word completes the blank in this sentence? Yesterday, at the football game, we ____ in the bleachers. (sat)

Story and Comprehension Questions

Who sat on the float first?	Who was the last character to sit on the float?	Why did the pals decide to eat their ice cream on the float _outside_ the pool?

Dictation

Heart Word	and
Letters/Sounds/Rime Patterns	-at, -it, -im
Words	sat, sit, Tim
Sentence	Tim sat.

Target Skills for Game Plan

As students move from the Full Alphabetic/Decoding Phase of word recognition to the Partial Mapping Phase, they rely less on blending each letter sound to pronounce whole words and begin to automatically recognize larger units of language. Attention to larger word parts results in greater efficiency and automaticity in reading. The activities and instruction in the Game Plan are designed to develop the following two skills:

- Automatic decoding of two- and three-letter short vowel words (VC and CVC)
- Automatic spelling of two- and three-letter short vowel words (VC and CVC)

Your Team

Students are ready for this Game Plan once they can accurately identify short vowels and consonant sounds in isolation. Students at this phase of word recognition may rely too heavily on sounding out each word, which can hinder their overall reading fluency and affect their comprehension of the text.

Case Study

Matteo, a kindergartener, is accurate with his letter sounds in isolation and, with prompting, can slowly blend the sounds to form a word. Currently, he relies on the continuous blending strategy to decode words. On a measure of nonsense word fluency, he is able to meet benchmark expectations for correct letter sounds but is not yet automatic or fluent enough to meet the expectations for reading the whole word. What strategies can help Matteo become more fluent in both reading and spelling?

Your Equipment

Series: Dandelion Readers Set 3 Units 1-10
(ISBN 9780744095265)
Reader: *Sit on It* (Book 1)
Phonics Concept:
Rime pattern recognition
of two- and three-letter
short vowel words (VC
and CVC).
Book Overview:
A day at the pool serves
up refreshment and fun
for a group of friends.

Text from the Book *Sit on It*

Tim sat.

"Sam! Tam! Sit on it!"

Sam sat on it.

Tam sat on it!

Tam! Sam! Tim!

Tam, Tim, and Sam sat on it.

Additional Texts

The **Dandelion Readers Set 1 Units 1-10** (ISBN 9780744095135) and **Set 2 Units 1-10** (ISBN 9780744095258) follow the same scope and sequence as the **Dandelion Readers Set 3 Units 1-10**, thereby providing the opportunity for instruction and application in additional texts before moving on to the next set of letter–sound correspondences.

Planning for Game Day

The Game Plan in Chapter 2 was designed using the same backward planning approach as Chapter 1. Backward planning ensures the activities in the Structured Literacy routines are aligned with the patterns, vocabulary, and text students will encounter in the accompanying book. First, select the instructional focus area and a decodable text that will help reinforce the development of the targeted skills. From there, identify three sentences containing words with the target skill. These words will be used for phonemic awareness instruction, single word reading, dictation, and vocabulary. For the Letter/Sound/Rime Review, identify sounds that students need to blend together for single word reading. Finally, set a purpose for reading and craft a variety of questions that support reading comprehension. The sequence for backward planning is shared in the following breakout box on page 42.

Backward Planning Using a Decodable Text

Planning Reading Activities (Sentences, Single Words, and Letter Sounds)

Step 1: Choose three sentences from the text. Select sentences that offer practice for target phonics skills.

Step 2: Select four individual words that appear in the sentences for single word reading practice.

Step 3: Choose the letters and rime patterns from the single word practice to teach sound-symbol correspondence.

Planning Phonemic Awareness Activity

Use the words from the single word reading activity for phonemic awareness (blending).

Planning Heart Word and Dictation Activity

Step 1: Choose up to four heart words from the text.

Step 2: Select rime patterns, one heart word, three single words, and at least one sentence from the reading activities for dictation tasks.

Planning Vocabulary and Comprehension Activities

Step 1: Develop questions that inquire about the meanings of the single words previously practiced.

Step 2: Read the text and craft questions that require students to find the information in the text (factual questions), analyze word meaning (semantic questions), or "read between the lines" to understand the deeper purpose of the story (inference questions). Set a purpose for reading by asking students to keep a particular question in mind as they read the book.

Winning Strategies

The instructional routines in the Game Plan support the ongoing development of students' word recognition skills through four Winning Strategies:

- Recognizing rime patterns in words
- Backward decoding
- Strategic instruction for heart words
- Reinforcing word recognition through spelling

Recognizing Rime Patterns in Words

One of the largest and most consistent units in English words is called the rime pattern. A rime pattern consists of the vowel and any subsequent consonants within that word/syllable. In the word "sat," the rime pattern is "-at." The letters preceding the rime pattern are linguistically referred to as the onset, but throughout *The Structured Literacy Playbook*, the term "starter" will be used.

Instruction in rime patterns, sometimes referred to as analytic phonics, has been proven equally effective for young readers as the sound-by-sound synthetic approach (National Reading Panel (US), 2000). Rime pattern instruction is particularly helpful for developing sight word recognition for several reasons. First, it highlights a "chunk" of a word, as opposed to an individual letter; next, it encourages reading across the entire word (Kilpatrick, 2015); and finally, rime pattern instruction supports the correct pronunciation of the vowel. In English words, vowel sounds are controlled by the letters that follow them, not those that precede them. For example, the words below all begin with the letters 'be,' but the pronunciation of the vowel sound changes in each word, and this change is governed by the letters (or lack thereof) after the vowel 'e.'

Differences in Vowel Pronunciation Based on Rime Patterns in Words

be   best   beast   berate

Backward Decoding

Backward decoding is an effective instructional technique that supports partial orthographic mapping. During the process of backward decoding, students read the rime pattern before reading the starter sound. Although this backward approach may seem counterintuitive at first, reading words from back to front actually capitalizes on the cognitive processes used for word recognition. The ability to recognize words automatically without decoding relies on several underlying foundational skills, including a reader's auditory memory for sound sequences (Kilpatrick, 2015). Evidence indicates that humans store words in their auditory memory using two major phonological cues: the first sound and the rime pattern. Reading words by rime pattern is a practice that not only activates a student's auditory memory for all the words that they know with that pattern but also, as was noted earlier, supports students in producing the correct pronunciation of the vowel. For example, when students backward decode the word "went" by reading the rime pattern "-ent" first, all of the words in their auditory memory that contain a similar or matching rime pattern are activated (e.g. bent, sent, tent, went). When the starter sound is added to the rime pattern, the students are more likely to accurately pronounce and map the entire word.

Strategic Instruction for Heart Words

A significant proportion of words in the English language do not follow common phonetic rules. These words can be recognized by their irregular spelling patterns (for example, the, said, have, from). Words with irregular spelling patterns occur frequently in text and are therefore a common part of early literacy instruction. The terms that educators use for these words vary by the curriculum and may include "high-frequency words," "trick words," or "red words," to name a few. In *The Structured Literacy Playbook*, these commonly occurring irregular words are called heart words, and it is recommended that students are taught the related letter patterns for reading and spelling using a strategic approach called Heart Word Magic. Heart Word Magic was developed by Really Great Reading to support students' word analysis skills. The instructional approach is helpful in the way that it emphasizes using knowledge of traditional letter-sound relationships and while also noting irregular patterns (Really Great Reading, 2024). Utilizing a word's sound sequence and stressing the letter or letters that produce each sound has strong research-based support (Kilpatrick, 2020); it aids in students' overall ability to "map" the word for rapid recognition in the future.

Reinforcing Word Recognition Through Spelling

Strategic, explicit, and systematic dictation activities play a crucial role in literacy achievement. These activities go beyond mere memorization; they focus on developing understanding of phonetic patterns, spelling rules, and morphophonemic structures within language (Galuschka et al, 2020). When instruction is systematic, students are guided in a step-by-step manner. This process ensures that each skill builds logically upon the previous one, helping to prevent gaps in foundational knowledge. Systematic spelling practice reinforces the connections between sounds and letters, enabling students to decode and encode more effectively (Graham & Santangelo, 2014).

Moreover, these structured activities foster students' phonemic awareness, allowing them to distinguish and manipulate sounds—a core skill in reading and writing fluency. Dictation activities that are aligned with the sounds, single words, and sentences from their text offer a dual benefit. They help reinforce the correct pronunciation and spelling of words in context. Over time, this cohesive approach offers reciprocal benefits to students: spelling skills are enhanced by reading achievement, and reading achievement strengthens spelling automaticity and accuracy.

Simultaneous Oral Spelling Strategy (SOS)

Simultaneous Oral Spelling (SOS) is a multisensory teaching procedure used to help students improve their spelling. By saying each sound in the word aloud and visualizing each letter before writing it down, students connect the phonological, visual, and auditory processes needed for accurate spelling. The SOS steps are below.

1. Teacher says the word for spelling.
2. Students repeat the word.
3. Starting with the thumb, students sound out the word, holding up one finger for each sound. (Students needing support might skip or add a sound. Use Elkonin boxes and counters or tokens to help the students visually represent each sound in the word.)
4. Starting with the thumb again, students now "finger spell" the word, holding up one finger for each letter. Make sure students are saying each letter out loud.
5. Students are now ready to write the word. Coach students to say each letter as they put pencil to paper.
6. Finally, students read the word aloud.

Executing Your Game Plan

→ Step 1: Maximize Phonemic Awareness Instruction

Our ability to recognize, identify, and manipulate individual sounds in spoken words is called phonemic awareness. Phonemic awareness activities that have high utility include blending and segmenting. These skills are the most closely related to our abilities to decode and encode. In the Game Plan, the words used in the phonemic awareness activities are pulled directly from the text and address the lesson's target phonics skills. If the text offers a limited selection of practice words, bolster your activity with additional words that follow your target pattern. See Chapter 1 (pages 24–26) for more about blending sounds.

Words for Phonemic Awareness Blending Activity in Game Plan

Sounds to Blend	Whole Word
/i/ /t/	it
/s/ /i/ /t/	sit
/t/ /i/ /m/	Tim
/a/ /t/	at
/s/ /a/ /t/	sat
/t/ /a/ /m/	Tam

Step 2: Teach Phonics Concepts Using Winning Strategies

The target phonics skills for the Game Plan are automatic decoding and spelling of two- and three-letter short vowel words (VC and CVC). In order to achieve these goals, the lesson incorporates two Winning Strategies that move students towards greater automaticity in recognizing letter pattern chunks: recognizing rime patterns in words and backward decoding.

Select several CVC words to use for instruction. Consider the skill level of your students. Students with the greatest level of need will benefit from a tightly controlled lesson in which a limited number of words are used for modeling and practice. The Teacher Scripts that follow on pages 47 and 48 are designed for students who know the consonants 's,' 'p,' 'm,' 't,' and 'd,' as well as the vowels 'a' and 'i.'

WINNING STRATEGY: Recognizing Rime Patterns in Words

Rime pattern instruction is particularly helpful for developing sight word recognition for several reasons. First, it highlights a chunk of a word as opposed to an individual letter; next, it encourages reading across the entire word (Kilpatrick, 2020); and finally, rime pattern instruction supports the correct pronunciation of the vowel.

Most children are not familiar with strategies for either identifying or reading words by rime pattern. The first step for a teacher is introducing the universal presence of rime patterns in all English words. Then, work with students to support their independent ability to recognize the rime patterns in words. See the **Teacher Script for Recognizing Rime Patterns** on page 47 and the **Teacher Script for Practicing Backward Decoding** on page 48 for a model of how to introduce this strategy in a lesson.

Teacher Script for Recognizing Rime Patterns

Introduction to Strategy

Teacher: *Did you know that every word has at least one rime pattern? Rime patterns start with a vowel sound and usually end with consonant sounds. Let's practice underlining the rime pattern in a few words.*

Type of Words

Three-Letter Closed Syllable Short Vowel Words (CVC Words)

Teacher Language and Prompt for Modeling

Write "tip" on the board.

Teacher: *Let's find and underline our first rime pattern. I am going to run my finger under the letters of the first word. When I come to the letter making a vowel sound, put your hand in the air. (Stop when your finger reaches the vowel 'i.')*

Teacher: *This letter 'i' is making the vowel sound /i/. This is where our rime pattern starts. (Begin underline.) The rime pattern ends with the letter 'p.' (Conclude underline.) The rime pattern is "-ip." (Prompt students to repeat.) Now let's practice with a few more.*

Additional Practice

sip   mat   sad

 WINNING STRATEGY: Backward Decoding

Once students understand the concept of a rime pattern and can identify the rime pattern in a three-letter short vowel word (CVC), guidance is provided on reading words by rime pattern. This strategy is called backward decoding and increases the automaticity with which students recognize words.

In order to backward decode, students are instructed to first read the rime pattern, then pronounce the starter sound in isolation, and finally blend the sounds together to produce the entire word. During the Single Word Reading activity, apply the backward decoding technique to the single words from the Game Plan.

Introduction to Strategy

Teacher: *We have already practiced identifying and underlining the rime pattern. Now our rime pattern is going to help us read words more quickly. We are going to read the rime pattern first using a technique called backward decoding.*

Type of Words

Three-Letter Closed Syllable Short Vowel Words (CVC Words)

Teacher Language and Prompt for Modeling

Return to word list (tip, sip, mat, sad).

Teacher: *Let's look at the first word. We have already underlined the rime pattern. Now I am going to read the word starting with the rime pattern. Watch me. "-ip." When I say "rime pattern," you read the pattern. (Elicit "-ip.") Now I am going to read the starter sound. Watch me. "t-."*

Teacher: *When I say "starter sound," I want you to only read the starter sound. (Elicit "t-.") Now I am going to blend the two parts together. Watch me. "tip." When I say "blend," I want you to blend the starter sound and rime pattern. (Elicit "tip.") Now let's practice with a few more.*

Additional Practice

s<u>ad</u>: ad - s - sad

s<u>ip</u>: ip - s - sip

m<u>at</u>: at - m - mat

Step 3: Reinforce Letters/Sounds in Isolation

The Game Plan includes opportunities to practice identifying letters/rime patterns and corresponding sounds that appear in the text in isolation before reading them in words. Teaching familiar letter patterns such as rime units facilitates the recognition of word parts and enables greater automaticity in word recognition and spelling. The lesson features several different sounds to practice in isolation: two consonant starter sounds, /s/ and /t/, as well as the rime patterns "-at," "-am," "-it," and "-im." See **Letter/Sound/Rime Review for Game Plan** on page 49.

See Chapter 1 (page 28) for **Teacher Script for Introducing, Modeling, and Practicing Letter/Sound Review** as necessary. For guidance on practicing letter sounds and rime patterns in isolation, see the following teacher scripts.

Letter/Sound/Rime Review for Game Plan

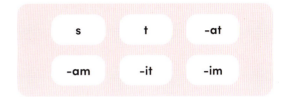

s	t	-at
-am	-it	-im

Teacher Script for Letter/Sound/Rime Review: Single Letters

Introduction to Strategy

Teacher: *We are going to review some letters and sounds to help us with our reading.*

Type of Letters

Choose individual consonants and vowels from the Game Plan.

Write the first letter to review on a whiteboard or utilize letter/sound cards from your curriculum resources.

Teacher: *The letter is ___. (Point to the letter and say the letter name.)*

Students repeat.

Teacher: *The sound to say is ___. (Point to the letter and say the sound.)*

Students repeat.

Continue with each letter.

If using letter/sound cards from a different curriculum, include keywords or images as needed.

Additional Practice

The Game Plan suggests reviewing six letters/letter patterns. You may choose to add additional letters for review, but keep in mind this portion of the routine should be brief.

Corrective Feedback

Since this activity is teacher-led, corrective feedback may not be necessary. To reduce the scaffolds, consider eliciting the letter name and/or sound as opposed to providing it for the students.

Teacher: *The letter is ___. (Point to the letter and elicit the name.)*

Students respond.

Teacher: *The sound to say is ___. (Point to the letter and elicit the sound.)*

Students respond.

Teacher Script for Letter/Sound/Rime Review: Rime Patterns

Introduction to Strategy

Teacher: *We are going to review some rime patterns to help us with our reading.*

Type of Letters

Choose rime patterns from the Game Plan or additional rime patterns to review.

Write the first rime pattern to review on a whiteboard.

Teacher: *The rime pattern is ___. (Point to the rime pattern and pronounce the rime pattern.) What's the rime pattern?*

Students respond.

Teacher: *The letters are ___. (Point to the rime pattern and name the letters.) What are the letters?*

Students repeat.

Continue with each letter.

If using letter/sound cards from a different curriculum, include keywords or images as needed.

Additional Practice

The Game Plan suggests up to six letters/rime patterns. You may choose to add additional letters/rime patterns for review, but keep in mind this portion of the routine should be brief.

Corrective Feedback

Since this activity is teacher-led, corrective feedback may not be necessary. To reduce the scaffolds, consider eliciting the rime pattern as opposed to providing it for the students.

Teacher: *The rime pattern is ___. (Point to the rime pattern and elicit the correct response.)*

Students respond.

Step 4: Apply Phonics Concept to Single Words from the Text

The Game Plan features four words from the story *Sit on It*. These are "sit," "sat," "Sam," and "Tim." These words provide practice reading three-letter short vowel words (CVC words) and applying the Winning Strategy of backward decoding.

Individual Words for Game Plan

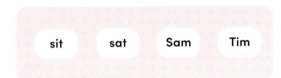

sit   sat   Sam   Tim

Read the Single Words Using Backward Decoding

Now that students understand the concept of backward decoding, instruct them in using the strategy with individual words from the text. Refer to the **Teacher Script for Practicing Backward Decoding** in Step 2 for guidance on coaching students with the backward decoding approach. As you practice, reduce the teacher language and provide short prompts that elicit choral responses from your students. Reducing teacher language and increasing unison responses affords students multiple opportunities to practice, which maximizes skill development.

Step 5: Build Knowledge of Heart Words

Most texts contain frequently occurring "tricky" words that break the rules of phonics and are challenging to decode. The Game Plans refer to these as heart words, because the tricky part must be learned by heart. As students progress through phonics instruction, the list of heart words often changes. For example, before students learn the vowel-consonant-e (VCe) pattern, the words "fine," "rope," and "Pete" are heart words, but only temporarily. Students will eventually learn the phonics rules for these words. Other heart words can be considered permanent, as they break all phonics rules. Permanent heart words include "said," "where," and "some."

In the Game Plan for this chapter, the word "and" from the story *Sit on It* is a temporary heart word. Students may have been taught the phonics rule for a nasalized version of the short vowel 'a' as /an/. If your student has been taught this phonics rule, then the word "and" would not be considered a temporary heart word. In this case, teachers can utilize their curriculum as a resource for determining additional words for instruction, or they may select alternate heart words from the series recommended for this chapter.

Selected Heart Words from Dandelion Readers Series Organized by Sound and Irregular Spelling

Title	Sound 1	Sound 2	Text
Pip, Sam, and Tam	/i/	/z/	Tam **is** on top of Sam. Pip **is** on top of Tam. Pip **is** not on top. Tam **is** not on top.
	i	s	

Title	Sound 1	Sound 2	Text
Pip, Sam, and Tam	/u/	/v/	Pip is on top **of** Tam.
	o	f	

Depending on the scope and sequence of your phonics program, your students may have already been taught the phonics patterns in certain temporary heart words. If that is the case, you may choose an additional word or simply use the strategy as a spelling review and do not use the heart.

WINNING STRATEGY: Strategic Instruction for Heart Words

The heart word strategy for learning irregular words capitalizes on the idea that each heart word has only one or two irregular spelling features. Rather than instructing a student to memorize the whole word, heart word instruction provides a strategy that emphasizes segmenting the sounds in the word, producing the phonetically regular spellings for sounds, and memorizing the one or two irregularly spelled sounds. This Winning Strategy will help students in identifying these tricky words by capitalizing on the aspects of the words that are familiar and drawing attention to those parts that need to be remembered by heart.

Teacher Script for Modeling and Practicing Reading and Writing Heart Words

Introduction to Strategy

Teacher: *Some words we read in English do not follow the phonics patterns we have learned. We call these words heart words, and we will use a new strategy for learning to read and spell these words. Since the words are not following the rules, we have to remember part of their spelling by heart. Let me show you how it works.*

Type of Words

Choose high-frequency words that are irregularly spelled.

Teacher: *The heart word today is _____.* (Teacher writes the word on the board and uses the word in a sentence.) *Say _____.*

Students repeat the word.

Teacher: *_____ is spelled _____.* (Teacher spells out the word, and students write the word on an index card.) *The word _____ can be broken up into _____ sounds. For example, "said" can be broken up into three sounds: /s/ /e/ /d/.*

Teacher raises one finger for each sound. Students are taught to repeat the teacher, raising a finger up for each sound.

Teacher and Students: Draw one dash on the card for each sound in the word. Teacher coaches students to say the sounds as they draw each line.

Teacher: (Teacher points to first dash.) *Which letter is making the sound _____ (first sound)?* (Teacher and students write the letter on the first dash. Teacher continues until

arriving at the irregular part of the word.)

Teacher: (Points to dash for the irregular portion of word.) *This sound is ___, but in this word, _____ (repeat heart word), we spell the sound _____ with the letter(s) _____. This is what makes the word tricky. We have to remember these letters by heart, so I am going to draw a heart underneath.* (Teacher and student draw a heart under the dash and write the letter(s). Continue with the rest of the heart words.) *Let's read the heart word one more time.* (Students run their fingers under the word as they read it.) *What was the tricky part in _____?*

Students respond. Students add the index card to a card ring for later practice.

Additional Practice

Repeat procedure for additional words using the same prompts. The part of the word that is underlined is "irregular" and has to be memorized by heart.

Sound 1	Sound 2	Sound 3
/h/	/a/	/z/
h	a	**s**

Sound 1	Sound 2
/th/	/u/
th	**e**

Step 6: Practice Reading Sentences from the Text

The sentence reading portion of the lesson offers students an opportunity to practice integrating decoding, heart word, and sight word skills. By selecting sentences from the text as a platform for practice, students can preview elements of the text before attempting to read the whole book.

Sentences for Game Plan

"Sam! Tam! Sit on it!"

Sam sat on it.

Tam, Tim, and Sam sat on it.

Step 7: Expand Text-Related Vocabulary Knowledge

One key element of Structured Literacy routines is the integration of multiple aspects of word knowledge. This includes connecting knowledge about phonics with knowledge about word meaning. Several prominent theories of reading comprehension, including the Simple View of Reading (Gough & Tunmer, 1986) and the Reading Rope (Scarborough, 2001), highlight the fundamental role of vocabulary knowledge in reading achievement. By integrating a dedicated section for vocabulary instruction into each Game Plan, lessons support integrating a dedicated section for the development of sight word recognition, fluency, and comprehension. Instruction that enhances both students' breadth of vocabulary knowledge and the number of associations they have for individual words strengthens word retrieval and supports text comprehension.

The vocabulary activity utilized in the current chapter's Game Plan is the same as the activity utilized in Chapter 1 (page 31). In order to enhance students' knowledge of word meanings, teachers can review previously taught words and incorporate a variety of questions that prompt students to think about word meanings. Questions may include references to synonyms, antonyms, and characters in the story, or they may offer students opportunities to complete a sentence. Before the activity, display the words from the Single Word Reading portion of the Game Plan and lead students through a choral reading of the word list. See the table **Words and Questions for Vocabulary Activity** on page 55 for a demonstration of this activity in practice.

Words and Questions for Vocabulary Activity

Game Plan: *Sit on It*	Questions
Tim/Sam/Tam	Which words are names?
sit	Which word completes the blank in this sentence? I am tired and need to find a chair to ___ in.
sit	Which word is the opposite of stand? (sit)
sat	Which word completes the blank in this sentence? Yesterday, at the football game, we ___ in the bleachers.

Game Plan: *Pip, Sam, and Tam*	Questions
Pip	Which word is a name?
tip	Which word means to fall over?
not	Which word has a negative meaning?
top	Which word means the peak, or highest level?

Maximize the Participation of All Students

In order to maximize the engagement of all students during vocabulary instruction, teachers can pair students together and instruct them in a "turn-and-talk" protocol. Turn-and-talk protocols teach students to take turns sharing their ideas with each other.

Turn-and-talk is an efficient and effective engagement strategy as it means that 50 percent of students are simultaneously answering each question. Compared with hand-raising, in which one student answers each question, turn-and-talk maximizes opportunities for students to practice and learn with their peers.

How to Teach Kids to Turn-and-Talk

Early in elementary school, many students struggle with impulse control and have difficulty waiting their turn to share their thinking. One reason hand-raising has become a universal tool for student engagement is because it gives students something to do as they signal to the teacher that they have a thought to share. However, as effective as hand-raising is at supporting impulse control, it is limited as a strategy for engagement. Only a portion of each class engages in regular hand-raising, and often the students who need the most support are the least likely to voluntarily participate in individual practice in front of their peers.

In order to support turn-and-talk as an effective alternative to hand-raising, teachers may need to explicitly teach students partner routines. The following ideas can support initial partner routines:

1. Assign consistent partners for different types of instruction. For example, during ELA instruction, students are paired with their "fruit salad partner," but during math instruction, they are paired with someone else called their "dessert table partner." Assign each partner one of two roles (e.g. fruit salad partners are kiwis or melons; dessert table partners are sprinkles or cherries).

2. Model partner routines in front of the whole group with a low-risk conversation starter (e.g. kiwis tell melons their favorite color, etc.).

3. After practice, discuss what went well about the routine (e.g. turn-taking, quiet listening while partner speaks, keeping body quiet while partner speaks, facing partner and making eye contact as appropriate).

4. Continue to model, review, and adjust turn-and-talk routines as necessary.

Step 8: Putting It All Together for Text Reading and Comprehension

In the final activities of the Game Plan, students must consolidate phonics skills and strategies, taught in isolation, to connected text. Before, during, and after reading, students' comprehension is supported through a series of questions that support the connection between word reading and meaning-making. Prior to beginning reading, activate students' background knowledge about the text by reading the title, discussing the cover, and previewing the content. In order to support comprehension monitoring, set a purpose for reading by posing one of the comprehension questions (e.g. "As we read, I want you to figure out the problem that our main character, _____, encounters in the book," or "Let's read to find out what happens to _____.").

Comprehension Questions for Game Plan

Factual
Who sat on the float first?

Factual
Who was the last character to sit on the float?

Inferential
Why did the pals decide to eat their ice cream on the float *outside* the pool?

Text from the Book *Sit on It*

Tim sat.

"Sam! Tam! Sit on it!"

Sam sat on it.

Tam sat on it!

Tam! Sam! Tim!

Tam, Tim, and Sam sat on it.

Use Choral or Partner Reading Instead of Round Robin

Maximizing student engagement and participation ensures all students have adequate opportunities to build their reading skills. See Chapter 1 (page 32) to learn more about the three primary engagement techniques for book reading: choral reading, partner reading, and reading to oneself.

Comprehension Questions

The comprehension questions developed for the Game Plans in this chapter focus on two aspects of text knowledge: factual knowledge and inferential knowledge. Factual questions are designed to support the recall and organization of specific information from the text. Inferential questions are designed to support students' analysis of text, integrating facts from the story and background knowledge to provide rationale or explanations for behavior.

Step 9: Applying Phonics Knowledge to Dictation

Although spelling patterns in English often feel nonsystematic and rife with irregularities, approximately 50 percent of words in English can be spelled using common phonics rules, and an additional 30 percent have only one sound with an irregular spelling (Moats & Tolman, 2009). Therefore, reinforcing common phonics rules through instructional routines that simultaneously practice key patterns in reading and spelling will increase the likelihood of consolidation and application among students. For example, learning to spell words enhances students' knowledge of the sound-symbol relationships that build sight word recognition, and when students spell words with phonics patterns targeted in their Structured Literacy routines, it enhances their decoding abilities (Graham et al, 2002; Moats, 2020).

Dictation Routine for Game Plan

Dictation	Selected Elements
Heart Word	and
Letters/Sounds/ Rime Patterns	-at, -it, -im
Words	sat, sit, Tim
Sentence	Tim sat.

WINNING STRATEGY: Reinforcing Word Recognition Through Spelling

Guided dictation is a Winning Strategy that supports both students' encoding and decoding skills. When it comes to planning the dictation portion, select an array of the sounds, words, heart words, and sentences included in the Game Plan's reading activities. For the current Game Plan, the dictation activity includes one heart word, three individual sounds or rime patterns to spell, three words that feature the target phonics skills, and one sentence. At times, it is necessary to simplify the sentence for dictation. In the current lesson, the sentence "Tam, Tim, and Sam sat on it" can be changed from the original text to the dictation version, "Tim sat." Sentence adjustments will vary depending on the students' needs and the options from the text. Another common modification for dictation sentences is replacing pronouns with character names (e.g. "He sat"/"Tim sat"). Practicing spelling characters' names helps reinforce the target phonics concept.

The dictation portion of the Game Plan is a wonderful opportunity to systematically teach the building blocks of spelling procedures in manageable increments. The sequence of activities moves from smaller to larger units of language, starting with sounds and words, then building to sentences. Furthermore, students are asked to spell sounds, words, and sentences on the final day of the lesson sequence. By this time, they have already completed half a dozen reading activities with the same sounds, words, and sentences. (See **Dictation Routine for Game Plan** on page 58.)

The dictation routine also offers an opportunity to provide explicit instruction in effective spelling strategies. Strategic spelling initially segments words into their smallest sound components. For example, breaking up a base word and its suffix, dividing syllables, or segmenting sounds. The letter(s) to spell each sound are then retrieved, and spelling rules are considered. The dictation approach is a modified version of Simultaneous Oral Spelling (SOS), a multisensory teaching procedure used to help students improve their spelling. By pronouncing each sound and corresponding letter before writing them down, students connect the phonological, visual, and auditory processes needed for accurate spelling. The following **Teacher Script for Dictation with Corrective Feedback** on page 60 includes suggested teacher language for the routine. If your phonics curriculum has a dictation routine, feel free to utilize those resources in that portion of the routine.

Teacher Script for Dictation with Corrective Feedback

Introduction to Strategy

Teacher: *Now we are going to spell some sounds, rime patterns, words, and write a sentence.*

Dictation of Heart Words

Teacher: *Your heart word to spell is _____.*
Students repeat the word.
The teacher can reinforce the Heart Word Magic strategy by identifying the number of sounds in the word and matching up the letters.

Prompt students as necessary.

Teacher: *How many sounds do you hear? What letter or letters represent that sound? Which letter or letters do we need to remember by heart?*

Corrective Feedback

If students incorrectly write the spelling for a sound or miss a letter (for example, if for the word "the" they write "tha"), use this script:

Teacher: *What's the word you are spelling?*
Student says word.
Have the student say the sounds and point to the letters that spell each sound.

When the student points to the incorrect letter(s), use this script:

Teacher: *You said _____. _____ is spelled _____ in the word _____.*
Student corrects misspelling.
Have the student say the sounds and point to the letters again to reinforce the correct spelling.
Students respond.

Dictation of Letters/Rime Patterns

For vowels and consonants:

Teacher: *The sound is ___. (Students repeat the sound.)*

Teacher: *What letter or letters make that sound?*
Students say and write the letter or letters.

For rime patterns:

Teacher: *The rime pattern is _____.*
Students repeat rime pattern.

Teacher: *What letters make the rime pattern?*
Students say and write the letters.

Corrective Feedback

If students respond incorrectly, use this script:

Teacher: *The sound (or rime pattern) is ___, and the letters that make that sound are _____.*
Students repeat.

Dictation of Single Words

Teacher: *The word is _____. (Use the word in a sentence.)*
Students repeat the word.
Teacher: *Tell me the starter sound in _____.*
Students provide.
Teacher: *What letter or letters make the starter sound?*
Students say and write the letter or letters.
Teacher: *Tell me the rime pattern in _____.*
Students provide.

Teacher: *What letters make the rime pattern?*
Students say and write the letters.
Teacher: *Read the word back to yourself and check that your letters match your sounds.*

This is a scaffolded approach. You can provide more or less support, depending on your students.

Corrective Feedback

If students respond incorrectly, use this script:

Teacher: *The sound (or rime pattern) is ____, and the letters that make that sound are ___.*
Students repeat.

Dictation of Sentences

Teacher: *The sentence is _____. Now, I am going to throw you the sentence. Hold your pencil in your writing hand and catch the sentence in your other hand.*
Mimic throwing the sentence, saying it again as you "throw" the words to the students.
Teacher: *Let the sentence out of your hand, putting up one finger for each word.*

Students follow the procedure, and the teacher ensures they have all of the words in the sentence.

After students have written the whole sentence, have them touch each word and read the sentence as they check for punctuation, missing words, or spelling errors.

Corrective Feedback

For sentences longer than five words, consider breaking them into phrases and dictating each phrase separately. If students have difficulty remembering the sentence, remind/show them how to use their fingers to say the words.

Some students benefit from an additional scaffold of drawing a line for each word.
If students do not notice an error, have them point and read the sentence again. Show them the word with the error. If necessary, have them say the word, the sounds in the word, and the letters that spell the sounds.

Proposed Practice Schedule

The nine-step routine outlined in this Game Plan is designed to be delivered over the course of several days. Delivering instruction in this manner not only creates a feasible schedule for teachers but also provides the opportunity for deliberate and spaced practice to support students in consolidating skills (Archer & Hughes, 2011). The practice schedule below provides suggestions for utilizing the Game Plan over the course of three days, in sessions ranging from 15–20 minutes. It should be noted that Day 1 does not include connected text practice. Providing daily opportunities to practice connected text is always preferable, so, if time permits, consider having students reread a familiar text from a previous lesson.

Day 1 (15 mins)	Day 2 (18 mins)	Day 3 (17 mins)
Phonemic Awareness (2 mins)	Building Knowledge of Heart Words (5 mins)	Book Reading and Comprehension Questions (7 mins)
Phonics Concept (5 mins)	Sentences (7 mins)	Dictation (10 mins)
Letter/Sound/Rime Review (3 mins)	Vocabulary (6 mins)	
Single Words (5 mins)		

Game Plan

Decodable Text: *Pip, Sam, and Tam*, Dandelion Readers Set 3 Units 1–10, Book 2

Phonics Concept: **Rime pattern recognition of two- and three-letter short vowel words (VC and CVC)**

Phonemic Awareness

not	top	tip
pit	Pip	Tam

Phonics Concept

Provide direct instruction in the phonics concept, utilizing words pulled from the Reader and/or that fit the patterns you are teaching.

Letter/Sound/Rime Review

t	–an	–op	–ot	–ip	–am

Single Word Reading

not	top	tip	Pip

Heart Words

of	is

Sentence Reading

Tam is on top of Sam.

Pip, Tam, and Sam tip.

Pip is not on top.

Vocabulary

Which word is a name? (Pip)	Which word means to fall over? (tip)	Which word has a negative meaning? (not)	Which word means the peak, or highest level? (top)

Story and Comprehension Questions

Who sat on top of Sam?	What happens when Pip gets on top?	Where did Pip, Sam, and Tam land?

Dictation

Heart Word	of
Letters/Sounds/Rime Patterns	–op, –ot, –ip
Words	not, top, tip
Sentence	Pip is not on top.

Chapter 3

Early Sight Word Development

- ⭘ Backward decoding with complex rime patterns

- ⭘ Utilizing RAN charts to build automaticity with single words and phrases

- ⭘ Developing word associations through vocabulary instruction

Game Plan

Phonemic Awareness

must	tent	went
dump	camp	junk

Phonics Concept

Provide direct instruction in the phonics concept, utilizing words pulled from the Reader and/or that fit the patterns you are teaching.

Letter/Sound/Rime Review

-amp	-ank	-ump	-ent	-ust	-unk

Single Word Reading

must	went	dump	camp

Heart Words

said	the	to	of

RAN Charts (Single Words & Phrases)

must	went	camp	dump	at the dump	off to camp	this old tent	I must
went	camp	dump	must	off to camp	this old tent	I must	at the dump
camp	must	went	dump	this old tent	off to camp	at the dump	I must
dump	went	camp	must	I must	at the dump	off to camp	this old tent

Sentence Reading

"I must get rid of this old tent," said Alf.

Alf met Hank at the dump.

Hank and Alf went off to camp.

Vocabulary: mend

Definition	Sentence	Questions
(v) To repair something.	My sister used her sewing kit to mend the hole in my shirt.	Why would you need to mend something? What tools can you use to mend? What is another word for mend?

Story & Comprehension Questions

What does Alf bring to the dump?	Why did Alf bring the tent to the dump?	In the story, Hank offers to mend a tent. What skills does Hank need to mend the tent? What other word means the same as "mend"?

Dictation

Heart Word	said
Letters/Sounds/Rime Patterns	-ust, -ent, -amp
Words	must, went, camp
Sentence	Alf met Hank at the dump.

Target Skills for Game Plan

In the Partial Mapping Phase of word recognition, students continue to build skills in order to become automatic in their ability to recognize larger units of language. When students are able to attend to larger word parts, such as consonant blends and rime patterns, they are more efficient in mapping and have greater automaticity in reading. Some students require additional instruction and practice opportunities in order to move to the final word recognition phase of reading, Consolidated Alphabetic/ Orthographic Mapping. The activities and instruction in the Game Plan aid in developing the following skill:

o   Automatic recognition of four-letter short vowel words with final consonant blends (CVCC)

Your Team

Students who are able to accurately blend sounds together to read three-letter short vowel words are ready for this lesson. Students may even be able to read some CVC words automatically or by rime pattern or be accurately blending the sounds for four-letter short vowel words. Typically, students achieve this skill at the mid-first-grade level. However, students at any phase or grade can benefit from these strategies if they still rely on sound-by-sound reading and have yet to build their "sight word vocabulary" to instantly recognize words as a whole unit.

Case Study

Sienna is in the middle of first grade and knows the letters and corresponding sounds of the alphabet. She can read and spell many CVC words and heart words with automaticity, but at times she resorts back to reading words sound by sound. Sienna's teacher has been meeting with her in a small group for several weeks. The instruction has focused on introducing backward decoding, or reading by rime pattern. Sienna's teacher reports she is utilizing this strategy in the small group but might benefit from additional practice in order to apply it independently to longer words. What strategies/activities can the teacher use to move Sienna towards more independence?

Resources for Skill Identification

Many students acquire the skills needed to read and spell VC and CVC words with strong whole class Structured Literacy, but they struggle when words become more complex (for example, when adding consonant blends at the beginning and end of short vowel words). As instruction increases in complexity, students' skills may begin to diverge, and some may require robust small group instruction. In order to plan and deliver instruction that meets students' needs, utilize materials to identify appropriate instructional focus areas. There are several resources available to educators; these include the scope and sequence of your core classroom instruction and/or diagnostic assessment tools such as phonics inventories.

Scope and Sequence from Classroom Curriculum

The scope and sequence from your classroom curriculum can be an effective tool for identifying a target skill when your students are only slightly below grade level and demonstrate similar learning needs/profiles. For example, after completing a unit on digraphs such as 'ch,' 'th,' and 'sh,' a small group of students continue to mispronounce the sound of short vowel /i/. This is a skill that was introduced and practiced in the previous unit. As you plan your small group intervention, focus on passages or books with plentiful opportunities to read short vowel /i/ words, rather than moving ahead in the scope and sequence to focus on digraphs.

Diagnostic Assessment/ Skill Inventories

Diagnostic tools are particularly helpful when there is a group of students with varying levels of ability. They are also useful in situations where an established phonics scope and sequence is unavailable. Diagnostic tools function as inventories in identifying skills that are "in stock" versus those that need to be taught or mastered. Most inventories present a collection of individual letter sounds, nonsense words, sight words, and sentences for students to read. Examiners tally the raw scores and analyze error patterns to determine target skills for instruction. Commonly used diagnostic inventories include the following: Quick Phonics Screener (Hasbrouck & Parker, 2006) and Beginning and Advanced Decoding Surveys (Really Great Reading, 2010).

 # Your Equipment

Series: Dandelion Launchers Stages 8-15
(ISBN 9781783693115)
Reader: *Junk* (Book 8a)
Phonics Concept:
Rime pattern recognition of short vowel words with final consonant blends (CVCC).

Book Overview:
Two strangers share common interests in upcycling and outdoor activities.

Text from the Book *Junk*

"I must get rid of this old tent," said Alf.

Alf went to the dump.

Alf met Hank at the dump.

"I can mend that old tent," said Hank.

"I can mend that old lamp," said Alf.

Hank and Alf went off to camp.

Additional Texts

Dandelion Launchers Extras Stages 8-15 (9780744095340) and **Dandelion World Stages 8-15** (9780744095920) follow the same scope and sequence as **Dandelion Launchers Stages 8-15**, thereby providing the opportunity for instruction in additional texts.

An additional Game Plan that targets similar skills and utilises another book from the **Dandelion Launchers Stages 8-15** series is available at the end of the chapter.

 # Planning for Game Day

The Game Plan for Chapter 3 was designed using a backward planning approach. Planning lessons with the end in mind—application of skills to connected text—ensures that skill-building activities in the Structured Literacy routines prioritize patterns, vocabulary, and text students will encounter in the accompanying book. The sequence for backward planning is shared in the following breakout box on page 69.

Backward Planning Using a Decodable Text

Planning Reading Activities (Sentences, Single Words, RAN Charts, and Letter Sounds)

Step 1: Choose three sentences from the text. Select sentences that offer practice for target phonics skills.

Step 2: Select four individual words that appear in the sentences for single word reading practice.

Step 3: To build RAN charts, use the four individual words and appropriate short phrases from the sentences.

Step 4: Choose letters and rime patterns from the single word practice to teach sound-symbol correspondence.

Planning Phonemic Awareness Activity

Use the words from the Single Word Reading activity for phonemic awareness (blending).

Planning Heart Word and Dictation Activity

Step 1: Choose up to four heart words from the text.

Step 2: Select rime patterns, one heart word, three single words, and at least one sentence from the reading activities for dictation tasks.

Planning Vocabulary and Comprehension Activities

Step 1: Select a high-utility word from the book and develop 'w' questions to elicit students' connections or associations.

Step 2: Read the text and craft questions that require students to find the information in the text (factual questions), analyze word meaning (semantic questions), or "read between the lines" to understand the deeper purpose of the text (inference questions). Set a purpose for reading by providing a question for students to keep in mind as they read the book.

Winning Strategies

The instructional routines in the Game Plan for this chapter support the ongoing development of students' word recognition skills. This is achieved through the utilization of the following three Winning Strategies:

- Backward decoding with complex rime patterns
- Utilizing RAN charts to build automaticity with single words and phrases
- Developing word associations through vocabulary instruction

Backward Decoding

One of the Winning Strategies covered in Chapter 2 (page 47) introduced students to the concept of reading by rime pattern, otherwise referred to as backward decoding. A rime pattern consists of the vowel and any subsequent consonants within that word, or in multisyllabic words, that syllable. For example, in the word "junk," the rime pattern is "-unk" and the starter, or onset, is 'j.'

Backward decoding is particularly effective as students move from reading three- to four-sound words. The new sound places additional cognitive demands on students' auditory memory. As a result, many children struggle to accurately sequence and pronounce four- and five-letter words. Common errors include omitting a sound (e.g. "but" for "bunt"), switching the position of sounds (e.g. "felt" for "left"), or mispronouncing sounds (e.g. "punt" for "pant"). Backward decoding reduces the frequency with which these errors occur by utilizing phonological, or auditory, memory. Phonological memory is part of the phonological processor, one of the four interconnected systems (e.g. phonological, orthographic, semantic, and contextual processors) that make meaning out of written language (Seidenberg & McClelland, 1989). Backward decoding with single-syllable words can provide the foundation necessary for students when they encounter words with more complex rime patterns, as well as words with two or more syllables.

Utilizing RAN Charts to Build Automaticity with Single Words and Phrases

As noted in Chapter 2, the use of rime pattern instruction supports students' ability to move away from decoding words one sound at a time and toward recognizing them as a whole unit. Rapid Automatic Naming (RAN) charts provide a repeated presentation of single words or phrases from the text. The use of a RAN chart offers several benefits. First, it provides an opportunity to practice the automatic retrieval of common single words and phrases. Second, it supports tracking across the page and the "return sweep" to the next line (Wolf & Katzir-Cohen, 2001). By incorporating backward decoding and the use of RAN charts, educators provide the scaffolds sometimes necessary to move students away from reading sound by sound and toward automatic recognition of words as a whole unit. Automatic word recognition, or "sight word recognition," indicates the word has been processed so efficiently by the student's reading circuit that it is now instantly recognizable, or orthographically mapped. The instant recognition of orthographically mapped words is essential for overall reading achievement. Decoding every word diminishes reading fluency and comprehension of text.

Developing Word Associations Through Vocabulary Instruction

Vocabulary instruction is an important element in building word recognition and fluency skills, as words with a greater number of associations are recognized more quickly in printed text (Pexman et al, 2008). There are several different features of word meaning that enhance associations and subsequent retrieval. Notably, vocabulary words that have more "semantic neighbors," or associations, that frequently co-occur in the same content are retrieved more quickly than words with fewer neighbors. For example, the word "pitch" co-occurs with words such as baseball, sports, player, sales, soccer field, throw, catch, southpaw, hand, glove, and ball. By contrast, the word "mulch" tends to co-occur with fewer words, such as garden, dirt, and leaves. Building the density of students' semantic neighborhoods is an important part of vocabulary instruction. In the Game Plan, vocabulary instruction combines explicit instruction and guided questioning designed to elicit experiences about the features of key vocabulary terms.

Executing Your Game Plan

Step 1: Maximize Phonemic Awareness Instruction

Our ability to recognize, identify, and manipulate individual sounds in spoken words is called phonemic awareness. Phonemic awareness activities that have high utility include blending and segmenting. These skills are the most closely related to our ability to decode and encode. In the Game Plan, the words used in the phonemic awareness activities are pulled directly from the text and address the lesson's target phonics skills. If the text offers a limited selection of practice words, bolster your activity with additional words that follow your target pattern. See Chapter 1 (pages 24–25) for the **Teacher Script for Introducing, Modeling, and Practicing Phonemic Awareness**.

Words for Phonemic Awareness Blending Activity in Game Plan

Sounds to Blend	Whole Word
/m/ /u/ /s/ /t/	must
/t/ /e/ /n/ /t/	tent
/w/ /e/ /n/ /t/	went
/d/ /u/ /m/ /p/	dump
/k/ /a/ /m/ /p/	camp
/j/ /u/ /n/ /k/	junk

Step 2: Teach Phonics Concepts Using Winning Strategies

The target phonics skill for the Game Plan is the automatic recognition of four-letter short vowel words with final consonant blends. Select several CVCC words from the decodable text to use for instruction in the Winning Strategies.

WINNING STRATEGY: Backward Decoding with Complex Rime Patterns

In order to achieve the Game Plan's phonics goal, the lesson incorporates the Winning Strategy of backward decoding. Backward decoding moves students towards greater automaticity in recognizing letter pattern chunks. During backward decoding, students are prompted to read words in the following sequence:

1. Pronounce the rime pattern
2. Pronounce the starter sound
3. Blend the starter and the rime pattern
4. Re-pronounce the whole word

Differentiating Instruction to Offer Increased Support

Some students may struggle to accurately read rime patterns that include two final consonant sounds. In these cases, teachers can break down the task in order to offer more incremental support. This process involves breaking up the final consonant blend and modeling reading the rime pattern with the first consonant, pronouncing the second consonant in isolation, then blending the entire rime pattern before adding the starter sound.

1. hunt:	/un/ – /t/ – /unt/ – /h/ – hunt
2. tent:	/en/ – /t/ – /ent/ – /t/ – tent
3. left:	/ef/ – /t/ – /eft/ – /l/ – left

Rebellious Rime Patterns

There are some English rime patterns in short vowel words that do not follow the rules. We call them rebellious rime patterns. The letter sounds rebel against short vowel conventions by making a long vowel sound or a distorted nasal vowel sound.

Step-by-Step Instruction for Teaching Rebellious Rime Patterns

Rebellious rime patterns should always be taught as a unit, as dividing them will elicit a mispronunciation of the vowel sound. Students benefit from explicit instruction with the pronunciation of rebellious rime patterns as they are unexpected and require additional explanation, modeling, and practice.

Teacher Script for Modeling and Practicing Backward Decoding with Complex Rime Patterns

Introduction to Strategy

Teacher: *Let's continue using our backward decoding strategy and reading words by rime pattern first. You might notice the rime patterns in these words are a little longer than we are used to. We have to teach our brains to read across longer words.*

Type of Words

Single-Syllable Short Vowel Words with Final Consonant Blends (CVCC Words)

Teacher Language and Prompt for Modeling

Write "such" and underline the rime pattern.

Teacher: *Watch me read the rime pattern: "-uch." Now I pronounce the starter sound: "s-." Finally, I blend them together: "such." I repeat the whole word: "such."*

Repeat the procedure with students, simplifying language.

Teacher: *Rime pattern. (Elicit "-uch.") Starter sound. (Elicit "s-.") Blend. (Elicit /s/ /u/ /ch/.) Whole word. (Elicit "such.")*

Additional Practice

Repeat the procedure for additional words using the same prompts. As a teacher, be sure to write the words without reading them aloud.

1. pick: /ick/ – /p/ – pick
2. sock: /ock/ – /s/ – sock
3. much: /uch/ – /m/ – much
4. gulp: /ulp/ – /g/ – gulp

Common Rebellious Rime Patterns

all – "fall"	ild – "child"	old – "cold"
am – "jam"	ind – "mind"	olt – "bolt"
an – "can"		ost – "most"
ang – "fang"		
ank – "tank"		

Teacher Script for Modeling and Practicing Backward Decoding with Rebellious Rime Patterns

Introduction to Strategy

Teacher: *Let's continue with reading words using backward decoding. Today, we are going to start learning about some patterns that "rebel," or break phonics rules we have been learning. We will call them rebellious rime patterns.*

Type of Words

Single-Syllable Short Vowel Words with Rebellious Rime Pattern (CVCC Words)

Teacher Language and Prompt for Modeling

Write the word "fall" on the board and underline the rime pattern "-all."

Teacher: *Our rebellious rime pattern today is A-L-L. The keyword to remember the pattern is "fall," and we pronounce the rime pattern as "-all." Now let's practice together.*

Teacher: *Letters.* (Elicit "A-L-L.")
Keyword. (Elicit "fall.")
Rime pattern. (Elicit "-all.")
Let's practice backward decoding words that contain our new rebellious rime pattern.

Additional Practice

Repeat the procedure for additional rebellious rime patterns using the same prompts. Suggested keywords and additional pattern practice items are included:

Rebellious Rime	Keyword	Additional Items for Practice
-all	fall	tall, mall, ball
-am	jam	ram, ham, Sam
-ind	mind	find, kind, bind
-old	cold	told, mold, bold

Step 3: Reinforce Letters/Sounds in Isolation

The Game Plan includes activities for practicing rime patterns. Teaching familiar letter patterns such as rime units enables greater automaticity in word recognition and spelling. The Game Plan features six rime patterns featured in decodable words in the story *Junk*. See Chapter 1 (page 28) for **Teacher Script for Introducing, Modeling, and Practicing Letter/Sound Review** as necessary.

Rime Patterns for Game Plan

-amp	-ank	-ump
-ent	-ust	-unk

Step 4: Apply Phonics Concept to Single Words from the Text

The Game Plan features four words from the story *Junk* and the sentences from which they have been taken. The rime patterns that comprise the selected words offer practice with the lesson's target phonics skill (i.e. reading short vowel words with final consonant blends). Apply the instructional language from the **Teacher Script for Modeling and Practicing Backward Decoding with Complex Rime Patterns** (page 73) to practice the single words from *Junk*.

Once your students have been introduced to the concept of backward decoding complex rime patterns (see page 72), you will want to provide ample opportunities for direct and explicit practice.

Individual Words for Game Plan

must	went	dump	camp

Step 5: Build Knowledge of Heart Words

The Game Plan for this chapter features four heart words from the decodable story *Junk*. See Chapter 2 (pages 52–53) for the **Teacher Script for Modeling and Practicing Reading and Writing Heart Words** if needed.

The format that teachers can use to demonstrate dividing the heart words by sound and the irregular aspect of the words is outlined below.

Heart Words for Game Plan

As a teacher, be sure to model breaking the words into sounds and matching letters for each sound. The part of the word indicated by the heart is "irregular" and therefore has to be memorized by heart.

said

Sound 1	Sound 2	Sound 3
/s/	/e/	/d/
s	**ai**	d

the

Sound 1	Sound 2
/th/	/u/
th	**e**

to

Sound 1	Sound 2
/t/	/oo/
t	**o**

of

Sound 1	Sound 2
/u/	/v/
o	**f**

Step 6: Enhance Sight Word Recognition with RAN Charts

The Game Plan features one RAN chart of single words and one chart of phrases. Both the single words and phrases have been practiced in earlier Game Plan activities. By providing a repeated presentation of these elements, the RAN charts offer a platform for enhancing sight word vocabulary through rapid recognition.

Maximizing Student Engagement with RAN Charts

The RAN charts in the Game Plan consist of both the individual words in isolation and short phrases from the sentences and text. RAN charts are intended to be read chorally to maximize the participation of all members of the group. Choral reading of RAN charts is achieved by displaying one copy of the chart, digitally or in print, and controlling the pacing of reading with nonverbal cues, or "sweeps," under the word or phrase. It may be helpful for teachers to use the scripts for RAN chart instruction and error correction on pages 78–79.

RAN Charts for Game Plan

at the dump	off to camp	this old tent	I must
off to camp	this old tent	I must	at the dump
this old tent	off to camp	at the dump	I must
I must	at the dump	off to camp	this old tent

must	went	camp	dump
went	camp	dump	must
camp	must	went	dump
dump	went	camp	must

WINNING STRATEGY: Utilizing RAN Charts to Build Automaticity with Single Words and Phrases

The RAN charts are used to reinforce automatic word recognition, and if students continue to decode words sound by sound when reading the RAN chart, educators may want to revisit individual word reading and backward decoding activities. RAN charts are common tools used in cognitive neuroscience to ascertain the rate at which individuals can pair symbols with their verbal language (Wolf & Denckla, 2005). A traditional RAN chart randomly presents an array of five different objects, letters, or numbers across a page in four or five consecutive rows. The time it takes an individual to name all the symbols is highly correlated with their overall reading rate, or fluency. When used with younger children, it is a helpful predictive measure and indicates risk of later challenges with reading fluency. Practicing traditional object, letter, or number RAN charts has no academic value. Yet, RAN charts populated with frequently occurring words, letter patterns, or common phrases provide the repetition and practice necessary for some students to develop automatic word retrieval skills as they read across a line of text (Wolf et al, 2009).

Teacher Script for Modeling and Practicing RAN Chart Reading with Corrective Feedback

Introduction to Strategy

Teacher: *Now we are going to see the words we have been reading individually repeated in the rows of this chart. We are going to read the chart together, and all our voices will blend like a chorus.*

RAN Chart Examples

must	went	camp	dump
went	camp	dump	must
camp	must	went	dump
dump	went	camp	must

at the dump	off to camp	this old tent	I must
off to camp	this old tent	I must	at the dump
this old tent	off to camp	at the dump	I must
I must	at the dump	off to camp	this old tent

Teacher Feedback

Teacher: *When I put my pointer to the left of the word/phrase, think of it in your head. When I scoop underneath, say it aloud. Watch me. (Demonstrate reading words/phrases in first three boxes.)*

Corrective Feedback

When students pronounce a word or phrase inaccurately on the RAN chart, provide immediate corrective feedback using the following sequence:

Teacher: *My turn. That word is _____.*
Your turn. (Elicit choral response from students accurately pronouncing the word.)

Then, move the pointer back two squares to provide another opportunity for correct pronunciation.

For persistent errors, teachers can reteach target phonics skills by modeling the strategy and offering plentiful opportunities for practice.

Tips for Differentiating RAN Chart Instruction

If the skills of your students vary significantly, then you may want to use some of the differentiation strategies listed below.

Color-Code a RAN Chart

One way to differentiate the RAN chart is by color-coding rows to align with students' needs. For example, students reading rows shaded red may benefit from complete word practice, while students reading from rows shaded yellow may be practicing individual letter sounds or rime patterns in isolation. It is most beneficial for each student to read at least two rows to practice the "return sweep," the eye movement that allows the reader to fixate on the next line of text.

It may be helpful to provide each student with their own copy of the RAN chart.

Customize a RAN Chart

Readers who are slowly building foundational skills may benefit from a simple RAN chart that includes one or two words and common letter patterns (for example, a common rime pattern) from those words.

must	went	camp	dump
went	camp	dump	must

Supporting Multilingual Students

After reading the first line of a RAN chart, it may be beneficial to review the meaning of each word by using them in sentences, displaying a related image or illustration, or asking students to pantomime their connection to the word.

Step 7: Practice Reading Sentences from the Text

The sentence reading portion of the lesson offers students an opportunity to practice integrating decoding, heart word, and sight word skills. By selecting sentences from the text as a platform for practice, students can preview elements of the story. Additionally, supported repeated reading of connected text aids with the development of fluency and prosody skills. The current Game Plan has selected the following sentences from the text *Junk* because they include words that have final consonant blends in the rime pattern (e.g. tent, must, dump, camp, Hank).

Sentences for Game Plan

"I must get rid of this old tent," said Alf.

Alf met Hank at the dump.

Hank and Alf went off to camp.

Step 8: Expand Text-Related Vocabulary Knowledge

The vocabulary activities incorporated into Game Plans support the development of word recognition and are related to the text. As noted in the earlier chapters, vocabulary instruction is an important element in building students' word recognition. The vocabulary instruction in this chapter shifts away from defining multiple words to increasing students' depth of knowledge about a single word. The word "mend" is used for all vocabulary discussion and questions in the current Game Plan.

Vocabulary Word for Game Plan

Vocabulary Term

mend

Student-Friendly Definition

To repair something. (verb)

Using the Term in a Sentence

My sister used her sewing kit to mend the hole in my shirt.

Questions for Discussion:

- Why would you need to mend something?
- What tools can you use to mend?
- What is another word for mend?

WINNING STRATEGY: Developing Word Associations Through Vocabulary Instruction

The number of associations students have for a single vocabulary word is often referred to as their "semantic neighborhood" (Buchanan et al, 1996). Uniformly dense neighborhoods are common among students with strong background knowledge or literacy exposure. Students may also possess uneven neighborhood density that is only clustered around certain topics or types of vocabulary. For example, some students know a great deal about baseball but have minimal knowledge about Africa. The density of a word's semantic neighborhood can be developed through a combination of explicit instruction and guided questioning designed to elicit experiences about the features of key vocabulary terms. Guided questions utilize keywords such as *who, what, when, where,* and *how* to elicit students' associations and support the visualization of the vocabulary word in real life.

Step-by-Step Approach to Developing Word Associations Through Vocabulary Instruction

In order to develop a robust semantic neighborhood for a word, follow a simple sequence. First, provide a child-friendly definition and illustration of the term. Then, present the word in context by featuring it in a sentence. Finally, engage students with questions that elicit and develop associations and enhance visualization and imagery (see **Suggested Teacher Language for Building Word Associations** on page 82 for examples). When used in combination, visualization and the development of rich semantic neighborhoods have a positive impact on automatic word retrieval (Yap et al, 2012).

Suggested Teacher Language for Building Word Associations

Vocabulary Term

rid

Student-Friendly Definition

To remove someone or something completely. (verb)

Using the Term in a Sentence

Alf wants to get rid of his old tent.

Questions for Discussion

- Have you ever gotten rid of old items?
- Why did you need to get rid of them?
- Where did you put them?

Vocabulary Term

tent

Student-Friendly Definition

A shelter that can be used for sleeping. It is usually made of fabric and held up with poles or ropes. (noun)

Using the Term in a Sentence

The tent kept our family dry while camping in the rain.

Questions for Discussion

- When do you use a tent?
- How does it feel to sleep inside a tent?
- What supplies might you have in a tent?
- Who or what might you want to keep out of a tent?

Selecting Vocabulary Words

Vocabulary selection for your Game Plan is often subjective. In a Structured Literacy routine, the primary criterion is choosing a word that exemplifies the target phonics concept. However, several other vocabulary options likely exist in your text. Teachers might select a word because it is related to other academic topics and supports continuity of learning. Other vocabulary choices may connect to the knowledge and experiences of your students. For example, students who live in cold climates with plenty of maple trees may be more familiar with a term such as "sap" than students who are only surrounded by palm trees. One helpful rule of thumb is selecting words that are commonly occurring in text and used across disciplines but not often utilized in spoken language. Such vocabulary has been called "Tier 2" (not to be confused with tiers of instruction in a "Multi-Tiered Systems of Support model") and is often unfamiliar to students but thought to be more utilitarian than content-specific vocabulary (Beck et al, 2013).

Step 9: Putting It All Together for Text Reading and Comprehension

Ultimately, building word recognition skills is a pathway to ensuring fluent reading and comprehension. Although decodable texts are short and often limited in content, the passages still present opportunities to practice multiple aspects of students' comprehension, including factual, inferential, and vocabulary knowledge. The following questions have been generated for the Game Plan.

Comprehension Questions for Game Plan

Factual
What does Alf bring to the dump?

Inferential
Why did Alf bring the tent to the dump?

Vocabulary in Context
In the story, Hank offers to mend a tent.
What skills does Hank need to mend the tent?
What other word means the same as "mend"?

Text from the Book *Junk*
"I must get rid of this old tent," said Alf.
Alf went to the dump.
Alf met Hank at the dump.
"I can mend that old tent," said Hank.
"I can mend that old lamp," said Alf.
Hank and Alf went off to camp.

For the book reading portion, see Chapter 1 (pages 29 and 32) to learn more about maximizing student engagement during this portion of the lesson.

Step 10: Applying Phonics Knowledge to Dictation

The development of spelling skills often lags behind the development of reading skills, and students benefit from the implementation of a comprehensive approach that simultaneously supports the development of phonics skills for both word reading and spelling (Graham, 2020).

In Chapter 2 (page 45), a modified Simultaneous Oral Spelling routine is introduced. This is a way for teachers to ensure that students are taught a strategic, incremental approach to spelling. The Teacher Scripts and recommendations for differentiated instruction from Chapter 2 can be referred to as needed. A selection of rime patterns, words, and sentences used for reading have been featured in the dictation portion of the Game Plan.

Dictation Routine for Game Plan

Dictation	Selected Elements
Heart Word	said
Letters/Sounds/ Rime Patterns	-ust, -ent, -amp
Words	must, went, camp
Sentence	Alf met Hank at the dump.

Proposed Practice Schedule

An instructional lesson with 10+ steps is logistically impossible for most teachers to deliver in one sitting. The practice schedule below suggests one method of arranging the activities into approximately 20-minute lessons over the course of three days. As the first day of the lesson does not include connected text practice, rereading previously learned sentences for a quick lesson warm-up is recommended.

Day 1 (20 mins)	Day 2 (22 mins)	Day 3 (20 mins)
Phonemic Awareness (2 mins)	Heart Words (5 mins)	RAN Chart—Phrases (5 mins)
Phonics Concept (5 mins)	Sentences (5 mins)	Dictation (10 mins)
Letter/Sound/Rime Review (3 mins)	Vocabulary (5 mins)	
Single Words (5 mins)	Book Reading (read portion/entire book) (7 mins)	Finish Book/ Read Another Book (5 mins)
RAN Chart—Single Words (5 mins)		

Game Plan

Phonemic Awareness

felt	gift	must
damp	hand	tank

Phonics Concept

Provide direct instruction in the phonics concept, utilizing words pulled from the Reader and/or that fit the patterns you are teaching.

Letter/Sound/Rime Review

-elt	–ift	–ust	-amp	-ank	-ad

Single Word Reading

felt	gift	damp	tank

RAN Charts (Single Words and Phrases)

felt	gift	damp	tank	the gift	with his hand	cold and damp	in a tank
gift	damp	tank	felt	with his hand	cold and damp	in a tank	the gift
damp	tank	felt	gift	cold and damp	in a tank	the gift	with his hand
tank	felt	gift	damp	in a tank	the gift	with his hand	cold and damp

Heart Words

you	cold	said	live

Sentence Reading

Alf felt the gift with his hand.

"It is cold and damp!" Alf said.

"It must live in a tank," said Dad.

Vocabulary: tank

Definition	Sentence	Questions
(n) A large receptacle for holding liquid (or gas), usually for animals to live in.	We need a tank for the three fish we just bought at the pet store.	What different animals live in tanks? What are some important things to consider when buying a tank for an animal?

Story and Comprehension Questions

How did Alf describe the gift his dad gave him?	What hint did Alf's dad give him?	When Alf is trying to guess the gift, he says it is cold and damp. What does the word "damp" mean?

Dictation

Heart Word	you
Letters/Sounds/Rime Patterns	-elt, –ift, -amp
Words	felt, gift, damp
Sentence	It must live in a tank.

Chapter 4

Building Stamina with Longer Words

- Backward decoding with initial consonant blends and digraphs

- Reading and spelling with suffix -s

- Expanding vocabulary knowledge with multiple-meaning words

Game Plan

Phonemic Awareness

chimp	branch	twin
stick	chum	Chip

Phonics Concept

Provide direct instruction in the phonics concept, utilizing words pulled from the Reader and/or that fit the patterns you are teaching.

Letter/Sound/Rime Review

br-	tw-	-imp	-anch	-ick	-unch

Suffix Review

–s

Single Word Reading

twin	chimps	branch	sticks

Heart Words

says	are	they	to

RAN Charts (Single Words and Phrases)

chimps	twin	branch	sticks	Chip and Chad	twin chimps	a big branch	best chums
twin	chimps	sticks	branch	twin chimps	best chums	Chip and Chad	a big branch
branch	sticks	chimps	twin	best chums	a big branch	twin chimps	Chip and Chad
sticks	branch	twin	chimps	a big branch	Chip and Chad	best chums	twin chimps

Sentence Reading

Chip and Chad are twin chimps.

Chip has a big branch to set up his bed.

"We are best chums as well as twins," Chip says.

Multiple-Meaning Word: stick

Definition 1
(n) A branch that has fallen off a tree.

Definition 2
(v) To attach one thing to another.

Questions
What does a stick feel like?
Where might you find sticks on the ground?
What activities can you do with sticks when camping?
What type of animal likes to chase a stick?
What do you need to stick wrapping paper to a present?
Describe a time when your fingers were sticking together.

Sentence 1
The little dog carried a long stick home in his mouth.

Sentence 2
I will stick my drawing to a cardboard mat in order to have it framed.

Story and Comprehension Questions

What does Chad use for his bed instead of slim twigs?

Why does Chip think a slim twig is unable to hold up a bed?

Chip says that he and Chad are twins and best chums. What does "chums" mean?

Dictation

Heart Word	says
Letters/Sounds/Rime Patterns	-unch, -anch, tw-
Words	chimps, branch, sticks
Sentence	Chip and Chad are twin chimps.

Target Skills for Game Plan

In Chapter 3, instruction focused on building students' reading skills as they move from the Full Alphabetic/Decoding Phase to automatically recognizing larger chunks of four-letter short vowel words. The ability to read words by larger chunks is referred to as Partial Mapping and serves as a critical midpoint as students move away from sound-by-sound reading to recognizing words instantaneously. In Chapter 4, this work continues with increasingly complex patterns and longer words. Increases in word length are due to several factors. These factors include the addition of consonant blends (e.g. bl, sp, st) or digraphs (e.g. ch, wh, sh) at the beginning of the word and the addition of suffixes at the end.

The activities and instruction in the Game Plan aid in developing the following skills:

- Automatic recognition of four- and five-letter short vowel words with initial consonant blends or digraphs
- Automatic recognition of all short vowel words with the addition of the suffix –s
- Spelling all short vowel words with the addition of the suffix –s

Your Team

Students are ready for this lesson structure when they are able to automatically recognize some short vowel rime patterns (-VC), including those that end with consonant blends (-VCC). Students should also be able to correctly pronounce consonant digraphs (e.g. ch, wh, sh) in isolation. Typically, students achieve this skill at the middle to end of first grade. However, students at any phase or grade will benefit from these strategies if they continue to rely on sound-by-sound reading and have yet to develop reading fluency with taught concepts.

Case Study

Jonah is a first grader who is developing his word reading skills. When reading CVC words, he is largely accurate, but his teacher notices that when Jonah encounters longer short vowel words, his reading becomes inaccurate. When words contain blends, he is able to segment the sounds correctly, but when he recodes individual sounds into a word, he is incorrect. Jonah also often leaves off the endings of words. When spelling, Jonah consistently omits consonant sounds that are part of a blend. What strategies/activities can help move Jonah toward more independence?

Your Equipment

Series: Dandelion Readers Set 2 Units 11-20
(ISBN 9780744095302)
Reader: *Twin Chimps*
(Book 11)
Phonics Concept:
Recognition of short
vowel words with initial
consonant blends or
digraphs (CCVC and
CCVCC); suffix –s.

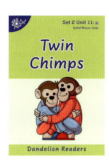

Book Overview: A pair of clever brothers
cooperate to build a home and enjoy a
tasty lunch.

Text from the Book *Twin Chimps*

Chip and Chad are twin chimps.

Chip has a big branch to set up his bed.

Chad has no big branch yet. He has six slim twigs.

"A slim twig will not hold up as a bed!" Chip says with a grin.

Chad has a plan.

"This bunch of twigs will be the best sticks to get bugs!" he tells Chip.

"Let's get a bug lunch!"

Chip and Chad get bugs with the twigs.

"Yum!" says Chip as they munch.

"That was the best lunch!"

It is dusk. Chip helps Chad get a big branch.

Chad sets his bed up next to Chip.

Chip and Chad hug and chat.

"We are best chums as well as twins," Chip says with a grin.

Additional Texts

An additional Game Plan
that targets similar skills and
utilizes another book from
the **Dandelion Readers Set
2 Units 11-20** series is
available at the end of
the chapter.

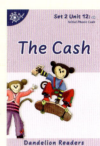

Planning for Game Day

The Game Plan in Chapter 4 was designed using the same backward planning approach as Chapters 1–3. Backward planning ensures the activities in the Structured Literacy routines are aligned with patterns, vocabulary, and text students will encounter in the accompanying book. The sequence for backward planning is shared in the breakout box on page 90.

Backward Planning Using a Decodable Text

Planning Reading Activities (Sentences, Single Words, RAN Charts, and Letter Sounds)

Step 1: Choose three sentences from the text. Select sentences that offer practice for target phonics skills.

Step 2: Select four individual words that appear in the sentences for single word reading practice.

Step 3: To build RAN charts, use the four individual words and appropriate short phrases from the sentences.

Step 4: Choose the letters and rime patterns from the single word practice to teach sound-symbol correspondence. In addition, include individual practice with the pronunciation of suffix -s.

Planning Phonemic Awareness Activity

Use the words from the Single Word Reading activity for phonemic awareness (blending).

Planning Heart Word and Dictation Activity

Step 1: Choose up to four heart words from the text.

Step 2: Select rime patterns, one heart word, three single words, and at least one sentence from the reading activities for dictation tasks.

Planning Vocabulary and Comprehension Activities

Step 1: Select a word with multiple meanings from the book and develop 'W' questions to elicit students' connections or associations with the multiple meanings.

Step 2: Read the text and craft questions that require students to find the information in the text (factual questions), analyze word meaning (semantic questions), or "read between the lines" to understand the deeper purpose of the text (inference questions). Set a purpose for reading by asking students to keep a particular question in mind as they read the book.

Winning Strategies

The Game Plan for this chapter, Building Stamina with Longer Words, includes the following three Winning Strategies to help students in this phase of reading:

- Backward decoding with initial consonant blends and digraphs
- Reading and spelling with suffix -s
- Expanding vocabulary knowledge with multiple-meaning words

Backward Decoding with Initial Consonant Blends and Digraphs

The backward decoding strategy is introduced in Chapter 2 (pages 43 and 47) with three-letter short vowel words (e.g. sad, sip, mat). It is expanded in Chapter 3 (pages 70 and 72) with four-letter words that contain rime patterns with blends (e.g. must, went) and digraphs (e.g. cash, with). The Game Plans in this chapter address the most complex short vowel words, these being four- and five-letter words that include initial consonant blends or digraphs and that may also incorporate blends or digraphs in the rime pattern (e.g. stick, twig, chimp). As words increase in length, additional cognitive demands are placed on the reader in order to sequence sounds correctly. Once words exceed three letters in length, some children struggle with accurate sequencing, and it can negatively impact their reading and/or spelling. For example, some students may sound out a word correctly (e.g. /s/ /p/ /l/ /a/ /t/) but mispronounce the whole word when they blend the sounds (e.g. spit). Others may spell the word but omit a letter (e.g. slat). Reinforcing students' ability to backward decode by pronouncing the rime pattern first and practicing the consonant blend or digraph as an isolated letter chunk supports both automatic word recognition and efficient spelling. For more information about backward decoding, see Chapters 2 and 3.

Reading and Spelling with Suffix -s

Prefixes and suffixes, collectively known as affixes, play a crucial role in developing word recognition and helping students to understand and expand their vocabulary. Students' knowledge about morphology not only supports their word recognition but also provides key information about the meaning and function of words in context. Morphology refers to the structure of meaningful word parts. These word parts are called morphemes. Morphemes fall into different categories: base words, prefixes, suffixes, and roots. Approximately 60–80 percent of multisyllabic words students encounter beyond second grade include prefixes and suffixes (Anglin et al, 1993). The addition of prefixes and suffixes increases the length of words. This increased length often acts as a bottleneck to reading achievement. Therefore, practicing the automatic recognition of morphemes supports reading fluency and aids with text comprehension. Teaching these word parts equips learners with tools that help them to decode unfamiliar words, enhancing their reading comprehension and writing skills. Understanding how to break down words into meaningful units allows students to deduce meaning from context, recognize patterns in word formation, and create new words themselves.

In the Game Plans, morphology instruction begins with suffixes. Suffixes are a more commonly occurring morpheme in foundational texts. The word suffix is a combination of the Latin prefix "sub," meaning "after," and the Latin root "figere," meaning "to fasten" or "to attach." When combined, "suffix" literally means "to fasten underneath" or "to attach after." This makes sense, as a suffix is attached to the end of a word.

Making Meaning of Morphemes

Morphology is the study of meaningful word parts. Individual word parts that carry meaning are called morphemes. One type of morpheme is an affix. Affixes are letter groups that carry meaning and, when attached to a base or root word, change its job or purpose. There are two categories of affixes, prefixes and suffixes.

- Prefixes are added to the beginning of a root word and modify its meaning (e.g. un- in "unhappy" means "not.")
- Suffixes are added to the end of a root word and often change the word's grammatical category (e.g. -ness in "happiness" turns an adjective into a noun).

Expanding Vocabulary Knowledge with Multiple-Meaning Words

The ability to automatically recognize words is not just based on the letters and sounds. Word recognition also recruits additional aspects of word knowledge. One primary aspect is word meaning. The beauty of Game Plans based on Structured Literacy is the inclusion of all aspects of word knowledge. Vocabulary knowledge refers to both the number of words students know and the depth of knowledge about individual words. Significant evidence points to the power of deep vocabulary knowledge as it relates to the speed of retrieval and overall reading fluency and comprehension (Carrier, 2011; Wright & Cervetti, 2017; Zipke et al, 2009). This is especially true for complex words, including those with multiple meanings (polysemous words). Nearly 75 percent of words children encounter will be polysemous (Zipf, 1945). The more frequent a word, the more likely it is to be polysemous.

Deep Vocabulary Processing Facilitates Comprehension

To use word knowledge for reading fluency and comprehension, students must efficiently retrieve a word's meaning and associations. Efficient retrieval is associated with a deep level of knowledge about the target word. When meaning is challenging to retrieve, the reader is forced to expend resources needed for comprehension. Words are more efficiently retrieved when they are robustly represented in the memory.

By incorporating instruction that highlights initial consonant blends, the recognition and meaning of foundational suffixes, and the multiple meanings of common vocabulary words, educators simultaneously support readers' stamina and comprehension.

Executing Your Game Plan

→ Step 1: Maximize Phonemic Awareness Instruction

Our ability to recognize, identify, and manipulate individual sounds in spoken words is called phonemic awareness. Phonemic awareness activities that have high utility include blending and segmenting. These skills are most closely related to our abilities to decode and encode. In the Game Plan, the words used in the phonemic awareness activities are pulled directly from the text and address the lesson's target phonics skills. If the text offers a limited selection of practice words, bolster your activity with additional words that follow your target pattern. See Chapter 1 (page 24) for **Teacher Script for Introducing, Modeling, and Practicing Phonemic Awareness**.

Words for Phonemic Awareness Blending Activity in Game Plan

Sounds to Blend	Whole Word
/ch/ /i/ /m/ /p/	chimp
/b/ /r/ /a/ /n/ /ch/	branch
/t/ /w/ /i/ /n/	twin
/s/ /t/ /i/ /k/	stick
/ch/ /u/ /m/	chum
/ch/ /i/ /p/	Chip

Step 2: Teach Phonics Concepts Using Winning Strategies

The target phonics skills for the Game Plan include the automatic decoding and spelling of four- and five-letter short vowel words with initial consonant blends or digraphs. Select several CCVC and CCVCC words from the decodable text to use for instruction in the Winning Strategies.

 WINNING STRATEGY: Backward Decoding with Initial Consonant Blends and Digraphs

As students build foundational reading skills, texts begin to increase in complexity. One aspect of text complexity involves the expanding length of individual words in a text. Just as moving from three-sound to four-sound words places additional demands on students' auditory memory, words that begin with more than one sound can be difficult, or "sticky," because they place a sequencing burden on the reader. A word's onset, or starter, is composed of either a single consonant (e.g. fit, pump, wish), a digraph (e.g. ship, think, when), or a consonant blend (e.g. flash, blob, slip). Digraphs are two letters that are pronounced as one sound. There are a limited number of onset digraphs in English, and they include the following: sh, wh, th, ch, ph, kn, and wr. Consonant blends refer to two or more consonant sounds that are blended together. There are a larger number of consonant blends than digraphs, including bl, sl, pl, spl, br, tr, pr, dr, and sp.

Step-by-Step Instruction for Introducing Sticky Starters

Although linguists refer to the initial sound in a word as the onset, students are likely more familiar with the term "starter." Sticky Starters are more difficult to manage than regular starters because they contain several letters. Educators are encouraged to introduce students to the function of word parts by using child-friendly language. Teachers can introduce Sticky Starters by referencing previous work with single starters and rime patterns. Just as backward decoding supports the automatic recognition of words with single starters, as discussed in Chapters 2 and 3, the technique will also build efficiency as students read words with Sticky Starters. The backward decoding strategy for Sticky Starter words demonstrates how to break up words into larger chunks. First, students are instructed to read the rime pattern, then pronounce the Sticky Starter in isolation. Next, they are prompted to blend the two word parts. Finally, they are instructed to re-pronounce the whole word.

Teacher Script for Introducing and Practicing Sticky Starters

Introduction to Strategy

Teacher: *We have been practicing reading by rime pattern and adding a single consonant at the start. Today we will practice adding blends, which we call Sticky Starters. To be a Sticky Starter, you need at least two consonants that stick close together and blend their sounds.*

Type of Words

Single-Syllable Short Vowel Words with Consonant Blends at the Beginning (CCVC and CCVCC Words)

Teacher Language and Prompt for Modeling

Write "ap."

Teacher: *Rime pattern.* (Elicit "-ap.")

Write "cl."

Teacher: *This is our Sticky Starter, "cl-." When I want you to pronounce the Sticky Starter, I will prompt you. Let's practice. Sticky Starter.* (Elicit "cl-.")

Teacher: *Next, we blend the Sticky Starter and rime pattern to say the word. My turn.*
"Clap." Now your turn. Blend the parts. (Elicit "clap.") *Finally, we say the whole word again. My turn. "Clap." Your turn.* (Elicit "clap.")

→ Step 3: Reinforce Letters/Sounds in Isolation

In order to help students build accuracy and automaticity in matching letters to their corresponding sounds, Game Plans include activities for practicing consonants, vowels, digraphs, blends, rime patterns, and affixes in isolation. Teaching familiar letter patterns such as rime units, consonant blends, and affixes facilitates the recognition of word parts and enables greater automaticity in word recognition and spelling. The Game Plan features the isolated practice of Sticky Starters and rime patterns featured in the story *Twin Chimps*. See Chapter 1 (page 28) for the **Teacher Script for Introducing, Modeling, and Practicing Letter/Sound Review** as necessary.

Letter/Sound Review for Game Plan

br-	tw-	-imp	-anch	-ick	-unch

Connection between Suffixes and Syntax

It is difficult to teach the pronunciation and purpose of word parts without first reviewing what students know about syntax and parts of speech. Affixes, particularly suffixes, tend to affect the parts of speech, or the jobs words play, in sentences. Prior to introducing words with suffixes, offer a child-friendly mini-lesson on parts of speech. A mini-lesson provides clarity and ensures all students have the same understanding of the "jobs" words have in a sentence. Here you can find a succinct explanation of the parts of speech that can be used in your mini-lesson.

Definitions and Examples of Basic Parts of Speech for a Mini-Lesson

Part of Speech	Definition	Examples from Text
Noun	A word that names a person, place, thing, or animal.	Chip, twig, chimp, branch, Chad
Verb	A word that names an action.	set, plan, get, munch
Adjective	A word that describes a noun.	big, slim, best

Step 4: Teach and Practice with Suffixes

One target phonics skill for the Game Plan is the automatic decoding and spelling of short vowel words with suffix -s.

WINNING STRATEGY: Reading and Spelling with Suffix -s

Introducing the pronunciation and purpose of suffixes is often best achieved by utilizing students' knowledge of oral language. This process entails drawing a comparison between the meaning of an independent base word and the meaning of a base word that has a suffix attached. Instruction commonly begins with suffixes because they are a more common affix in foundational texts.

Step-by-Step Instruction for Introducing Suffix -s

Once students understand parts of speech, educators can discuss the purpose of affixes and introduce the first suffix, -s. For example, a teacher might offer the following explanation: "Suffixes are word parts that have the power to change the meaning of the base word. Suffixes are found at the end of the word, and the word 'suffix' comes from the Latin words that mean 'attach after.' Some suffixes change the base word in one way, while other suffixes have the power to change the base word in different ways."

Each subsequent suffix is initially introduced by spelling and pronunciation, and then the meaning or meanings of the suffix are explained. By providing explicit, systematic instruction about affixes, all students are offered clarity about the purpose, pronunciation, and spelling of these important word parts. For specific teacher language, see the **Teacher Script to Introduce Suffix -s with Nouns** on page 98 and the **Teacher Script to Introduce Suffix -s with Verbs** on page 99.

Wait to Teach the Second Meaning of Suffix -s

It is recommended that you wait at least one day before teaching students the other way suffix -s can change the meaning of the base word. Otherwise, students might become confused.

Parts of Speech Can Be Tricky

Students' understanding of parts of speech will likely evolve as they move through elementary school. Multiple-meaning words that can function as both nouns and verbs are often tricky for first graders to discern. Mastery in this area is not necessary to continue with instruction in affixes. Educators are encouraged to continue weaving in discussions about parts of speech. Chapter 6 (pages 151–152) provides more depth on breaking up sentences into their phrasing structures with a technique called Syntactic Phrasing.

Teacher Script to Introduce the Suffix -s with Nouns

Introduction to Strategy

Teacher: *Today, I want to introduce you to a word part. These word parts can be attached to base words, and they have the power to change the meaning and pronunciation of the base word. The word parts we will be learning about are called suffixes. "Suffix" is a Latin word that means "attached after." Let me show you how it works.*

Type of Words

Single-Syllable Short Vowel Words with Initial Consonant Blends or Digraphs (CCVC or CCVCC Words) + Suffix -s

Introduce Spelling and Pronunciation of Suffix -s

Write -s on the board.

Teacher: *Here is the suffix -s. It is pronounced /s/ and sometimes /z/.* (Elicit correct pronunciation.)

Reading Nouns with Suffix -s

Teacher: *Suffix -s has two jobs. The first job of suffix -s is changing a single noun into a plural noun (i.e. more than one).* (Elicit correct pronunciation.)
Write "chimp."

Teacher: *What is our base word?* (Elicit "chimp.")
When we see the word "chimp," we think of one animal.

Add suffix -s to the base word "chimp" to get "chimps."

Teacher: *Notice that I attached the suffix -s at the end of the base word. The 's' changes the meaning of the base word to more than one. We no longer imagine one single chimp all alone. Now we think of a whole troop of chimps. Let's practice with a few more words.*

Additional Practice

1. twig + s = twigs

2. bug + s = bugs

3. bed + s = beds

Teacher Script to Introduce the Suffix -s with Verbs

Introduction to Strategy

Teacher: *Today, we will continue our discussion of suffixes. These word parts can be attached to base words, and they have the power to change the meaning and pronunciation of the base word.*

Type of Words

Single-Syllable Short Vowel Words with Initial Consonant Blends or Digraphs (CCVC or CCVCC Words) + Suffix -s

Introduce Spelling and Pronunciation of Suffix -s

Write -s on the board.

Teacher: *Here is the suffix -s. It is pronounced /s/ and sometimes /z/.* (Elicit correct pronunciation.)

Teacher: *Let's review the first job of suffix -s.*

Write "chimp" and "chimps" on the board.
The first job of suffix -s is to make a single noun into a _____. (Elicit "plural.")

Reading Verbs with Suffix -s

Teacher: *The second job of suffix -s is changing a verb into an action that one person is doing right now.*

Write "Tim and Tam run."

Teacher: *What does our sentence say?* (Elicit "Tim and Tam run."). *When I read that sentence, I picture two people running.*

Write "My dad run."

Teacher: *What does our sentence say?* (Elicit "My dad run."). *That is an inaccurate sentence. In English,* *when one person is completing an action right now, we add suffix -s to the verb. Which word is the verb/action?* (Elicit "run.")

Add the suffix -s to the verb. The sentence should now read "My dad runs."

Teacher: *Now let's practice with a few more. I will write an inaccurate sentence. You name the verb that needs the suffix -s to be accurate.*

Step 5: Apply Phonics Concept to Single Words from the Text

The Game Plan features four words from the text *Twin Chimps*. Each word includes at least one of the target skills—initial consonant blends or digraphs and/or the suffix -s.

Individual Words for Game Plan

twin chimps branch sticks

Step-by-Step Instruction for Reading Words with Sticky Starters or Digraphs and Suffix -s

Single word reading instruction, including words with suffixes, always begins by backward decoding the rime pattern. This approach is an efficient way to read words by chunks and results in greater fluency and accuracy. Students should wait to read the suffix until they have fully pronounced the base word. Following this sequence, students circle or ignore the suffix and first read the rime pattern. Then, students pronounce the Sticky Starter or digraph in isolation, blend the two word parts, and repronounce the base word. The final step is pronouncing the combined form of the base word and suffix. (See page 101 for **Teacher Script for Backward Decoding Sticky Starter Words from the Text**.) If it is more appropriate for you to teach words with single starters, you may want to refer back to Chapter 2 for backward decoding recommendations and script.

WINNING STRATEGY: Backward Decoding with Initial Consonant Blends or Digraphs and Suffix -s

Ongoing use of the backward decoding strategy with short vowel words that contain a Sticky Starter, consonant blend, and/or suffix -s supports the development of automaticity and accuracy with longer words.

Teacher Script for Backward Decoding Sticky Starter Words from the Text

Introduction to Strategy

Teacher: *We have been practicing reading by rime pattern and adding a single consonant at the start. Today we will practice adding blends, which we call Sticky Starters. To be a Sticky Starter, you need at least two consonants that stick close together and blend their sounds.*

Type of Word

Short Vowel Words with Sticky Starters (CCVC and CCVCC Words)	Short Vowel Words with Sticky Starters or Digraphs and Suffixes

Teacher Language and Prompt for Modeling

Write "in."

Teacher: *Rime pattern.* (Elicit "-in.")

Write "tw."

Teacher: *This is our Sticky Starter, "tw-." When I want you to pronounce the Sticky Starter, I will prompt you. Let's practice.*
Sticky Starter. (Elicit "tw-.")
Next, we blend the Sticky Starter and rime pattern to say the word. My turn. "twin."
Now your turn. (Elicit "twin.")
Finally, we say the whole word again.
My turn. "twin."
Your turn. (Elicit "twin.")

Write "chimps."

Teacher: *This word has a suffix -s. I am going to circle the suffix and save reading it until we have figured out our base word.*
Let's look at the base word. Rime pattern. (Elicit "-imp.")
Sticky Starter. (Elicit "ch-.")
Blend the sounds. (Elicit "chimp.")
Repeat the base word. (Elicit "chimp.")
Pronounce the suffix. (Elicit "-s.")
Combine the suffix and base word. (Elicit "chimps.")

Additional Practice

Example: **sticks**

1: Teacher writes "sticks."

2: Teacher circles suffix -s.

3: Teacher says "pattern"; students say "-ick."

4: Teacher says "Sticky Starter"; students say "st-."

5: Teacher says "blend"; students say "stick."

6: Teacher says "Repeat the base word"; students say "stick."

7: Teacher says "Suffix?"; students say "-s."

8: Teacher says "Whole word?"; students say "sticks."

Differentiating Instruction for Greater Support

There are a few key phonics rules to keep in mind when reading words with Sticky Starters; namely, how to differentiate instruction for students who struggle with accurate or automatic blending of the entire Sticky Starter and how to teach digraphs. See **Teacher Script for Differentiating Backward Decoding with Sticky Starters**.

Differentiating Instruction to Break Up the Consonant Blend

Differentiating instruction to break up the consonant blend is appropriate when students struggle to accurately produce the initial blend. Using the backward decoding method, educators sequence word reading to activate auditory memory for known words. In order to sequence efficiently, present the rime pattern, then add the consonant closest to the rime pattern, and finally blend the initial consonant with the rest of the word. For example, in the word "stick," present "-ick" (rime pattern), then "tick," and finally read "stick." This methodology preserves the form of the word in students' auditory memory and allows them to leverage the sequence of sounds for mapping the letter patterns accurately (Kilpatrick, 2020). (See the following **Teacher Script for Differentiating Backward Decoding with Sticky Starters** for additional guidance.)

Digraph Starters

Digraph starters are never split, because the letters in a digraph are no longer individually discernable; rather, they are coarticulated into one sound.

Teacher Script for Differentiating Backward Decoding with Sticky Starters

Reading Words with Entire Sticky Starter

Example: stick

1: Teacher writes "ick"; students say "-ick."

2: Teacher adds letters "st"; students say "st-."

3: Teacher says "blend"; students say "stick."

4: Teacher prompts "Whole word?"; students say "stick."

Reading Words One Consonant at a Time

Example: stick

1: Teacher writes "ick"; students say "-ick."

2: Teacher adds letter "t"; students say "tick."

3: Teacher adds letter "s"; students say "stick."

4: Teacher prompts "Whole word?"; students say "stick."

→ Step 6: Heart Words

Almost every text contains frequently occurring "tricky" words that break the rules of phonics and are impossible to decode. The Game Plan features four heart words from the story *Twin Chimps*.

The heart word strategy for learning irregular words capitalizes on the idea that each heart word has only one or two irregular spelling features. Rather than instructing a student to memorize the whole word, heart word instruction provides a strategy that emphasizes segmenting the sounds in the word, producing the phonetically regular spellings for sounds, and memorizing the one or two irregularly spelled sounds.

Each heart word in the Game Plan for *Twin Chimps* is divided into sounds in the table titled **Heart Words for Game Plan**. The part of the word that is irregularly spelled is identified with a heart. For scripting on teaching heart words, see Chapter 2 (pages 52–53).

Heart Words for Game Plan

As a teacher, be sure to model breaking the words into sounds and matching letters for each sound. The part of the word indicated by the heart is "irregular" and has to be memorized by heart.

s<u>ay</u>s

Sound 1	Sound 2	Sound 3
/s/	/e/	/z/
s	**ay**	s

<u>are</u>

Sound 1
/ar/
are

th<u>ey</u>

Sound 1	Sound 2
/th/	/ae/
th	**ey**

t<u>o</u>

Sound 1	Sound 2
/t/	/oo/
t	**o**

Step 7: Enhance Sight Word Recognition with RAN Charts

The Game Plan RAN charts include the individual words and phrases featured in other parts of the lesson. These frequently occurring words, letter patterns, and common phrases provide the repetition and practice necessary for some students to develop automatic word retrieval skills as they read across a line of text (Wolf et al, 2009). For guidance on teaching a RAN chart and differentiating instruction as needed, refer to Chapter 3 (pages 77–79).

RAN Charts for Game Plan

Chip and Chad	twin chimps	a big branch	best chums
twin chimps	best chums	Chip and Chad	a big branch
best chums	a big branch	twin chimps	Chip and Chad
a big branch	Chip and Chad	best chums	twin chimps

chimps	twin	branch	sticks
twin	chimps	sticks	branch
branch	sticks	chimps	twin
sticks	branch	twin	chimps

Step 8: Practice Reading Sentences from the Text

The Game Plan has selected the following sentences from the text *Twin Chimps* because they include words that contain Sticky Starters or digraphs (e.g. Chip, Chad, branch, twin), and/or suffix -s (e.g. chimps, chums, twins). These phonics concepts are the target skills for the lesson and the selected text offers plenty of opportunity for students to apply their word recognition strategies and develop fluency and comprehension.

Sentences for Game Plan

> Chip and Chad are twin chimps.
>
> Chad has a big branch to set up his bed.
>
> "We are best chums as well as twins," Chip says.

Adjusting Sentences to Support Comprehension

As you select your sentences, consider the following:

1. Include sentences in your lesson that offer plentiful opportunities to practice the target skill(s).
2. Select a variety of sentence lengths and styles to support skill generalization (for example, sentences with and without dialogue).
3. Choose sentences that are simple to comprehend as standalone statements. That may require replacing pronouns with proper nouns (e.g. replace "he" with "Chad").

Step 9: Expand Text-Related Vocabulary Knowledge

The vocabulary activities incorporated into the Game Plan support the development of word recognition skills by deepening students' knowledge of multiple-meaning words. Deep vocabulary knowledge enhances reading fluency, speed of retrieval, and comprehension. Fluent readers retrieve word meanings quickly and accurately. When retrieval is challenging, it detracts from comprehension. Efficient retrieval is linked to well-established connections between different aspects of word knowledge, including word meanings and associations (Pexman et al, 2008).

105

Vocabulary Word for Game Plan

Vocabulary Term

stick

Student-Friendly Definition 1

A branch that has fallen off a tree. (noun)

Using the Term in a Sentence

The little dog carried a long stick home in his mouth.

Student-Friendly Definition 2

To attach one thing to another. (verb)

Using the Term in a Sentence

I will stick my drawing to a cardboard mat in order to have it framed.

Questions for Discussion

- What does a stick feel like?
- Where might you find sticks on the ground?
- What activities can you do with sticks when camping?
- What type of animal likes to chase a stick?
- What do you need to stick wrapping paper to a present?
- Describe a time when your fingers were sticking together.

WINNING STRATEGY:
Expanding Vocabulary Knowledge with Multiple-Meaning Words

The word "stick" is used for vocabulary instruction in the current Game Plan because it is a multiple-meaning word and contains the target phonics patterns. Commonly occurring one-syllable short vowel words are useful for deepening students' word associations as they frequently have more than one meaning. See the table **Common Short Vowel Multiple-Meaning Words** on page 107.

Vocabulary knowledge expands through a hierarchy of knowledge development that begins with limited familiarity and develops to comprehensive knowledge (Beck et al, 2013).

Common Short Vowel Multiple-Meaning Words

back	bill	cap	duck	flop	jig	left	pen	sack	tip
bag	bit	cast	dust	glass	kid	mat	pitch	shed	top
band	blank	check	fish	gum	land	mint	pump	sink	tot
bank	block	deck	flat	hit	lash	mop	quit	slab	trunk
bash	camp	dip	flap	hog	last	pack	ring	sting	web
bat	can	dish	flip	hot	lap	pass	run	tab	well

Teacher Language and Prompt for Modeling

The mechanism by which students develop their levels of vocabulary knowledge is a combination of explicit instruction and active processing (Wright & Cervetti, 2017).

Levels of Vocabulary Knowledge	
Generating Contextual Use	Using the word in a new sentence or text
Receptive Contextual Use	Understanding the word's meaning in a sentence; offering an antonym; correctly identifying examples and non-examples of the vocabulary word
Limited Knowledge	Identifying the basic definition of a vocabulary word

Explicit Instruction

As multiple-meaning vocabulary words are introduced, explicit instruction is characterized by child-friendly definitions and associated sentences, as well as illustrations of meaning.

Active Processing

Active processing of word meanings is accomplished by eliciting students' associations with words and asking them to analyze scenarios where the word serves as appropriate terminology. By posing guided questions that probe when, where, who, what, and how students have experienced the word, educators elicit students' associations.

The conversational nature of vocabulary instruction lends itself to partner, small group, or whole class dialogue, where individual students can benefit from the collective experiences of their classmates. For example, since "stick" can mean "adhere," classmates can discuss the various tools available to make objects stick, such as glue and tape. The benefits of sticking paper together instead of stapling or using a paper clip can also be explored. The essential principle is that the more associations students can connect to a word, personal or relational, the greater their automaticity when retrieving its meanings and roles in text (Pexman et al, 2008).

Step 10: Putting It All Together for Text Reading and Comprehension

Ultimately, building word recognition skills is a pathway to ensuring fluent reading and comprehension. Although decodable texts are short and often limited in content, the passages still present opportunities to practice multiple aspects of students' comprehension, including factual, inferential, and vocabulary knowledge.

A series of comprehension questions have been developed to assess different aspects of students' understanding. (For guidance on whole group, choral, or partner reading and strategies teachers can employ to activate background knowledge and set a purpose for reading, see Chapters 2 and 3.)

Comprehension Questions for Game Plan

Factual
What does Chad use for his bed instead of slim twigs?

Inferential
Why does Chip think a slim twig is unable to hold up a bed?

Vocabulary in Context
In the story, Chip says that he and Chad are twins and best chums. What does the word "chums" mean?

Text from the Book *Twin Chimps*

Chip and Chad are twin chimps.

Chip has a big branch to set up his bed.

Chad has no big branch yet. He has six slim twigs.

"A slim twig will not hold up as a bed!" Chip says with a grin.

Chad has a plan.

"This bunch of twigs will be the best sticks to get bugs!" he tells Chip.

"Let's get a bug lunch!"

Chip and Chad get bugs with the twigs.

"Yum!" says Chip as they munch.

"That was the best lunch!"

It is dusk. Chip helps Chad get a big branch.

Chad sets his bed up next to Chip.

Chip and Chad hug and chat.

"We are best chums as well as twins," Chip says with a grin.

→ Step 11: Applying Phonics Knowledge to Dictation

A selection of words and sentences from the text Twin Chimps have been used to plan the dictation routine. Dictation serves as an additional learning opportunity to solidify skills through instruction, rather than serving as an assessment. Suggested language for completing the dictation exercise can be found in Chapter 2 (pages 60–61). If your phonics curriculum has a dictation routine, feel free to utilize those resources in that portion of the routine.

Dictation Routine for Game Plan

Dictation	Selected Elements
Heart Word	says
Letters/Sounds/Rime Patterns	-unch, -anch, tw-
Words	chimps, branch, sticks
Sentence	Chip and Chad are twin chimps.

Proposed Practice Schedule

The practice schedule below suggests one method of arranging the activities into approximately 20-minute lessons over the course of three days. Please note that the first day of the lesson does not include connected text, which is a high-leverage activity for building fluency, and we recommend rereading previously learned sentences for a quick lesson warm-up.

Day 1 (18 mins)	Day 2 (23 mins)	Day 3 (20 mins)
Phonics (5 mins)	Heart Words (5 mins)	RAN Chart—Phrases (5 mins)
Letter Sounds (3 mins)	Sentences (5 mins)	Dictation (10 mins)
Single Words (5 mins)	Vocabulary (8 mins)	Finish Book/Read Another Book (5 mins)
RAN Chart—Single Words (5 mins)	Book Reading (5 mins)	

Game Plan

Phonemic Awareness

stop	spend	spent
shelf	drink	best

Phonics Concept

Provide direct instruction in the phonics concept, utilizing words pulled from the Reader and/or that fit the patterns you are teaching.

Letter/Sound/Rime Review

-op	-end	-ent	-elf	-ash	-am

Suffix Review

-s

Single Word Reading

shelf	spends	spent	shop

Heart Words

from	says	you	has

RAN Charts (Single Words and Phrases)

shelf	spends	spent	shop	at the best shop	from the shelf	spends the cash	Sam stops
shop	shelf	spends	spent	Sam stops	at the best shop	from the shelf	spends the cash
spent	shop	shelf	spends	spends the cash	Sam stops	at the best shop	from the shelf
spends	spent	shop	shelf	from the shelf	spends the cash	Sam stops	at the best shop

Sentence Reading

Sam stops at the best shop.

Sam gets red gum from the shelf and spends the cash.

"But we spent the cash," says Tam.

Multiple-Meaning Word: spend

Definition 1	Definition 2	Questions
(v) Paying money for things you want or need.	(v) Using your time or energy to do something.	What are some things that you spend money on? What are some things you spend your time doing?
Sentence 1 During the holiday season, people spend a lot of money.	**Sentence 2** This weekend, I plan to spend some time reorganizing my bedroom.	

Story and Comprehension Questions

Why does Mom give Tam and Sam a list?	Why can't Tam and Sam get the items on Mom's list?	One of the items on the shopping list is jam. What does "jam" mean here? How might another meaning of "jam" describe the children's situation?

Dictation

Heart Word	from
Letters/Sounds/Rime Patterns	-op, -ent, -elf
Words	shop, spends, shelf
Sentence	Sam gets gum from the shelf.

Chapter 5

Decoding Multisyllabic Words

- Syllable division for multisyllabic short vowel words

- Spelling rules for words with suffix -s and -es

- Backward decoding multisyllabic short vowel words

- Spelling rules for multisyllabic short vowel words

Game Plan

Decodable Text: *The Sandpit*, Dandelion Launchers Stages 16–20, Book 17a
Phonics Concept: Reading and spelling multisyllabic words with short vowel syllables; syllable division; suffix -s/-es

Letter/Sound/Rime Review

-ish	-atch	-oth
-ick	-and	-um

Phonics Concept

Provide direct instruction in the phonics concept, utilizing words pulled from the Reader and/or that fit the patterns you are teaching.

Suffix Review

-s	-es

Single Word Reading

dishcloth	picnic	drumstick	sandwich

Heart Words

island	have	give	says

RAN Charts (Single Words and Phrases)

picnic	dishcloth	sandwich	drumstick	has a dishcloth	grabs her lunchbox	Meg snatches	the drumstick
picnic	sandwich	drumstick	dishcloth	grabs her lunchbox	has a dishcloth	the drumstick	Meg snatches
sandwich	drumstick	dishcloth	picnic	Meg snatches	the drumstick	has a dishcloth	grabs her lunchbox
dishcloth	picnic	drumstick	sandwich	the drumstick	grabs her lunchbox	Meg snatches	has a dishcloth

Sentence Reading

Viv has a dishcloth with a skull on it.

"Let's have a picnic on the island," says Viv and grabs her lunchbox.

Just then, Meg snatches the drumstick!

Multiple-Meaning Word: drumstick

		Questions
Definition 1 (n) The lower part of the leg of a chicken, which is cooked and eaten.	**Definition 2** (n) Sticks used for making music on a drum.	When might someone eat a drumstick? What type of musician might use drumsticks? How does it sound when drumsticks hit a drum?
Sentence 1 We will have drumsticks and mashed potatoes for dinner tonight.	**Sentence 2** My brother got new drumsticks in music class.	

Story and Comprehension Questions

What are Fred and Viv doing in the sandpit?	Why does Meg run off with the drumstick?	What does the word "bandit" mean?

Dictation

Heart Word	island
Letters/Sounds/Rime Patterns	-ish, -atch, -oth
Words	dishcloth, picnic, drumstick
Sentence	Meg snatches the drumstick.

In practice, RAN phrases should be displayed across a single line.

Target Skills for Game Plan

As students encounter increasingly sophisticated text, they will need guidance in reading a broader range of words, including multisyllabic words and those with suffixes. Effective teaching and recognition of multisyllabic words combines strategic instruction with purposeful practice opportunities. Instruction is characterized by strategies that break down longer words into efficient chunks and the integration of practice opportunities that support the application of skills to text. Additional activities offer guidance with spelling rules, connections to word meaning, and support for reading comprehension. Along these lines, the activities and instruction in the Game Plan are designed to develop the following two skills:

- Decoding and spelling multisyllabic words with short vowel sounds
- Spelling with suffix -es

Together, these instructional elements not only support students' accuracy in reading longer words but also build their automaticity, fluency, and comprehension.

Your Team

Students are ready for this lesson when they are able to automatically recognize one-syllable short vowel words with initial blends. Word length might range between four and six letters (e.g. span, sprint). Typically, students achieve this skill in the middle of first grade. However, students at any phase or grade will benefit from explicit instruction and guided practice if they continue to read words sound by sound or if they generally struggle with reading fluency.

Case Study

Geoff, eight years old, continues to struggle with accurately reading long words in text. When he encounters a long word, he tends to guess based on the context of the text or even the first letter of the word. Geoff has significant background knowledge and often selects texts on topics that are familiar to him. Until recently, Geoff has been able to use his language skills and background knowledge as compensatory strategies. However, the new unit in science requires Geoff to read about a topic that is new to him, and he has struggled to understand the text and answer questions accurately. What strategies can help Geoff become accurate in both reading and spelling multisyllabic words?

Your Equipment

Series: Dandelion Launchers Stages 16-20
(ISBN 9781783693344)

Reader: *The Sandpit*
(Book 17a)

Phonics Concept:
Reading and spelling multisyllabic words with short vowel syllables; syllable division; suffix –s/–es.

Book Overview:
Friends enjoy an imaginary quest until their adventure is interrupted by a hungry puppy.

Text from the Book *The Sandpit*

Viv and Fred are in the sandpit.
"Let's pretend this is an island," says Viv.

Fred is a frogman. Viv has a dishcloth with a skull on it.

"Let's have a picnic on the island," says Viv and grabs her lunchbox.

Viv has a sandwich and a plum. Fred has chicken drumsticks.

"I'll give you a chicken leg for that plum."
Fred hands Viv the chicken leg.

Just then, Meg snatches the drumstick!
"Bandit!" yells Viv as Meg runs off.

Additional Texts

An additional Game Plan that targets similar skills and utilizes another book from the **Dandelion Launchers Stages 16-20** series is available at the end of the chapter.

Planning for Game Day

The Game Plan in Chapter 5 was designed using the same backward planning approach as Chapters 1–4. Backward planning ensures the activities in the Structured Literacy routines are aligned with patterns, vocabulary, and text students will encounter in the accompanying book. The sequence for backward planning is shared in the breakout box **Backward Planning Using a Decodable Text** on page 116. Note that the current Game Plan no longer includes phonemic awareness activities. The focus on lesson activities has now shifted to advanced decoding and word recognition. If your students require ongoing support in phonemic awareness skill building, refer to the guidance from Chapter 4 for aligning activities that involve "blending" sounds with the words and letter patterns encountered in the accompanying decodable text *The Sandpit*.

Backward Planning Using a Decodable Text

Planning Reading Activities (Sentences, Single Words, RAN Charts, Letter Sounds, and Suffixes)

Step 1: Choose three sentences from the text. Select sentences that offer practice for target phonics skills.

Step 2: Select four individual words that appear in the sentences for single word reading practice.

Step 3: To build RAN charts, use the four individual words and appropriate short phrases from the sentences.

Step 4: Choose the letters and rime patterns from the single word practice to teach sound-symbol correspondence. In addition, include individual practice with the pronunciation of suffix -s and -es.

Planning Heart Word and Dictation Activity

Step 1: Choose up to four heart words from the text.

Step 2: Select rime patterns, one heart word, three single words, and at least one sentence from the reading activities for dictation tasks.

Planning Vocabulary and Comprehension Activities

Step 1: Select a multiple-meaning word from the book and develop 'w' questions to elicit students' connection or associations with the multiple meanings.

Step 2: Read the story and craft questions that require students to find the information in the text (factual questions), analyze word meaning (semantic questions), or "read between the lines" to understand the deeper purpose of the story (inference questions). Set a purpose for reading by providing a question for students to keep in mind as they read the book.

Winning Strategies

The instructional routines in the Game Plan support developing students' reading and spelling of multisyllabic words and those with the suffix -s or -es through four Winning Strategies:

- Syllable division for multisyllabic short vowel words
- Spelling rules for words with suffix -s and -es
- Backward decoding multisyllabic short vowel words
- Spelling rules for multisyllabic short vowel words

Syllable Division for Multisyllabic Short Vowel Words

Learning to read in English can be challenging because of the varied pronunciation of vowel sounds. The pronunciation of a vowel is determined by a word's syllable type (for more information about syllables, see the breakout box **Syllables 101**). Once accurate pronunciation of a vowel sound in single-syllable words has been mastered, students are ready to move on to multi-syllable words.

Using a strategic approach to read multisyllabic words is critical for overall reading achievement. These are the skills that will serve students as they encounter new information. Many students become stuck at the single-syllable level, and rather than strategically sounding out longer words, they rely on compensatory strategies for guessing unknown words. The most common compensatory strategies involve guessing, either based on the first letter of the word, the overall appearance of the word, or the context in which the word is used (Kilpatrick, 2020). Most multisyllabic words can be decoded utilizing a few key syllable division strategies. These approaches break up the word into small units of letter patterns. Teaching and practicing syllable division methods ensures that students have a strategic approach as they encounter longer and/or unknown words.

Syllables 101

A syllable is a word or part of a word with one vowel sound. Every word in English is made up of at least one syllable. Determining the syllables in a word involves counting the number of vowel sounds, not the number of letters. For example, the word "read" is one syllable because the letters 'ea' only make one vowel sound, /ee/. Other single-syllable words include "soup," "bait," and "flout."

Spelling Rules for Words with Suffix -s and -es

English texts are full of words that contain prefixes and suffixes. Morphologically complex words make up more than half of the words in English. Approximately 60–80 percent of written words from third grade onward have multiple morphemes, including roots, prefixes, and suffixes (Anglin et al, 1993). Words with affixes are complex because they are both longer and often contain an additional syllable, or vowel sound, compared to the independent base word. For example, most nouns are made plural by adding one of two suffixes. Suffix -s is added to most words that end with either a consonant or a silent 'e.' When suffix -s is added, the number of syllables in the base word does not change (e.g. cat/cats; lake/lakes). In contrast, suffix -es also creates a plural form of the word, but in the process adds an additional syllable (e.g. crutch/crutches; flash/flashes). Suffix -es is used when words end with 's,' 'x,' 'z,' 'sh,' or 'ch' because they "hiss" at the end. When a word ends in a sound that hisses, the vowel 'e' is added to help with the clarity of pronunciation and ensure the plural suffix is clearly processed (Eide, 2012). The complexity of these rules necessitates explicit instruction for most students, certainly in spelling, if not reading, which serves as one of the Winning Strategies for the current Game Plan.

Backward Decoding Multisyllabic Short Vowel Words

Research on word recognition implies that when proficient readers encounter longer, multisyllabic words, they sound them out by chunks. For example, one study that examined efficient strategies for reading multisyllabic words divided students into two groups. Group 1 was presented with multisyllabic words one letter at a time. Each letter was in its correct position but flashed only briefly on the screen before the next letter appeared (e.g. f-a-n-t-a-s-t-i-c; t-r-u-m-p-e-t; d-i-s-g-u-s-t). The researchers calculated the amount of time required for participants to name the word they had just viewed. Generally, participants were able to correctly name the word, but only if the interval between the letter presentation was very short. When the interval exceeded even a few seconds, accurate reading became more elusive. In Group 2, the multisyllabic words were divided into syllable chunks, and the word was flashed on the screen one chunk at a time (e.g. fan-tas-tic, trum-pet, dis-gust). The participants in the second group could read the words with greater accuracy than the first group, even when the intervals between

syllables was lengthened by several seconds (Mewhort & Beal, 1977). The implications of these findings lay the groundwork for our syllable instruction, which guides readers not only to divide syllables but also to sound them out from the back to the front, thereby activating our auditory memory for common word chunks.

Number of Syllables	Example Words Divided by Syllable with Underlined Vowel Sound
1	I, bed, split, cone, place, corn, read, soup.
2	pi·lot, hot·dog, or·der, can·not, ba·by
3	per·sis·tent, a·ban·don, com·plic·ate
4	wa·ter·mel·on, es·tab·lish·ment, ac·a·dem·ic

Spelling Rules for Multisyllabic Short Vowel Words

Spelling is particularly challenging for many students because it requires the integration of several related skills, including phonemic awareness, phonics, handwriting, and memorization of irregular letter patterns. As words increase in length, spelling complexity increases. The current Game Plan introduces a consistent, multisensory routine that identifies the syllables, segments each sound in an individual syllable and represents them with letters, and supports independence and achievement in spelling.

Executing Your Game Plan

→ Step 1: Teach Phonics Concepts Using Winning Strategies

There are two target phonics skills for the Game Plan. The first target phonics skill is decoding and spelling multisyllabic words with short vowel sounds. The decoding strategy is discussed below, and the spelling strategy for spelling multisyllabic words is introduced in the dictation section of the Game Plan.

 WINNING STRATEGY: Syllable Division for Multisyllabic Short Vowel Words

One foundational component of phonics instruction involves the ability to identify, read, and spell the syllables found in most English words. Most single-syllable words are straightforward, with one vowel producing one sound (e.g. bed, split). Some single-syllable words have multiple vowels (e.g. read, soup) or R-controlled vowels producing one sound (e.g. corn, thwart). There are six syllable types in English, and each type of syllable shifts the vowel pronunciation (see **The Six Syllable Types in English** on page 120). Some syllable types in English are very common, while others are more rare. The most common syllable type is a closed syllable where the vowel sound is short (e.g. bed, spill, trap, block). Closed syllables can be found in slightly over 40 percent of English words (Stanback, 1992). Familiarity

with common closed syllables, particularly in longer multisyllabic words (e.g. can·not, es·tab·lish·ment), offers students a broadly generalizable strategy in the early phases of their reading development.

Introducing a Syllable

Instruction on decoding multisyllabic words begins with a clear and concise definition of a syllable and practice identifying and pronouncing the vowel sound. Syllables can be defined as words or parts of words with one vowel sound. Placing a dot under each letter that represents a vowel sound is an efficient method for visually representing the number of syllables in a word. However, in order to pronounce the vowel sound correctly, it is helpful to underline the rime pattern in the syllable. (See **Identifying Vowel Sound and Rime Pattern in Syllables** on page 120.) Additionally, reading by rime pattern offers a more efficient word recognition strategy compared to sound-by-sound decoding, as described in Chapter 2.

The Six Syllable Types in English

Syllable Type	Vowel Sound	Sample Single-Syllable Words	Sample Multi-Syllable Words
Closed	The vowel sound is short and closed in by consonant sounds.	mad, bed, cot	blank·et, tab·let, cot·ton
Open	The vowel sound is long and is not followed by a consonant.	do, she, go, be	cra·zy, u·nit, fo·cus
R-Controlled	The vowel sound is distorted by the letter 'r' that immediately follows.	corn, tart, bird, surf, her	cor·ner, car·pet, dir·ty
Vowel Team and Vowel Diphthong	In a vowel team, the two vowels work together to represent one of their long or short sounds (e.g. bread, oat). In a vowel diphthong, the vowels work together to make a unique sound (e.g. boy, bowl).	Vowel Team: float, bean, plain Vowel Diphthong: sour, moist, plow	Au·gust, oat·meal, don·key
VCe	The vowel sound is long and followed by a consonant and silent 'e.'	blame, Pete, chute, pose	sun·shine, pan·cake, side·walk
Consonant 'le'	This syllable type occurs at the end of words and has a consonant followed by an 'l' and silent 'e.'	N/A	sim·ple, tur·tle, i·ci·cle

(Stanback, 1992)

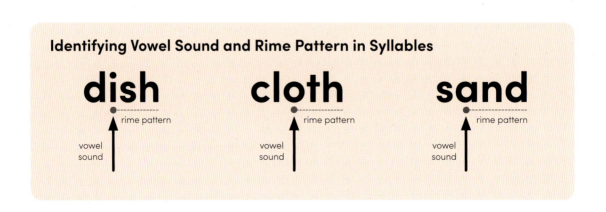

Identifying Vowel Sound and Rime Pattern in Syllables

dish
rime pattern
vowel sound

cloth
rime pattern
vowel sound

sand
rime pattern
vowel sound

Teacher Script to Introduce Syllables and Practice with Single-Syllable Words

Introduction to Strategy

Teacher: *All words are made up of syllables. Syllables are words or parts of words with one vowel sound. If you have one vowel sound in a word, you have one syllable. If you have two vowel sounds in a word, you have two syllables. If you have three vowel sounds in a word, you have _____ (elicit "three") syllables. Let's look at our list of words, find the vowel sounds, and count the syllables.*

Type of Word

Single-Syllable Short Vowel Words with Initial/Final Consonant Blends or Digraphs (CVCC, CVCCC, CCVC, or CCVCC Words)

Counting the Syllables by Finding the Vowel Sound

Write "dish" on the board.

Teacher: *I'm going to run my finger under the word. Put your hand in the air when I reach a letter that makes a vowel sound. (Stop at letter 'i.') We have found our vowel sound. The letter 'i' makes the sound /i/. I'm going to put a dot under the letter making a vowel sound. (Dot under 'i.')*

Teacher: *The dot will help us find our vowel sound and count our syllables. Are there any other letters that have a vowel sound in this word? (Elicit "no.") I am going to look for the dots to count the vowel sounds. (Count one dot.) We have one vowel sound, so this must be a one-syllable word.*

Identifying the Rime Pattern for Syllable Pronunciation

Teacher: *Even though we are discussing syllables, I don't want to forget about our rime patterns. Remember rime patterns are the groups of letters in a syllable that start with the vowel. Our vowel 'i' also starts our rime pattern "-ish."*

Teacher: *I'm going to underline the rime pattern. (Underline "ish.")*
Let's read the rime pattern. (Elicit "-ish.")
Now the whole word. (Elicit "dish.")
Now let's practice with a few more.

Dividing Multisyllabic Words

In order to accurately read multisyllabic words, students can follow a set of sequential strategies. First, find and dot the letter(s) representing vowel sounds. Second, identify and underline common rime patterns. Next, divide the syllables after the rime pattern. (See **Dot, Underline, and Divide between the Syllables**.)

1. *Dot the letters making vowel sounds.* Students dot under each letter making a vowel sound.
2. *Underline the rime pattern.* Find and underline the common rime patterns. In closed syllables where the vowel sound is short, rime patterns are composed of one vowel letter and one or two consonant letters (e.g. -VC as in "-ic" or -VCC as in "-ish").
3. *Divide the syllables.* Multisyllabic closed-syllable words are divided after the rime patterns. If there are double letters, divide the syllable between the letters (e.g. rab·bit).
4. *Read the syllables.* Once the word is accurately divided, correctly pronouncing the syllables involves retrieving the correct vowel sound and blending all the sounds in the correct sequence.
5. *Reread the whole word.* The final step is rereading the whole word as one unit.

Dot, Underline, and Divide between the Syllables

dish|cloth
rime pattern   rime pattern

pic|nic
rime pattern   rime pattern

drum|stick
rime pattern   rime pattern

sand|wich
rime pattern   rime pattern

Step 2: Reinforce Letters/Sounds in Isolation

The Game Plan includes activities for practicing rime patterns and affixes in isolation. Teaching familiar letter patterns such as rime units and affixes facilitates the recognition of word parts and enables greater automaticity in word recognition and spelling. The Game Plan features six rime patterns and two suffixes featured in the story *The Sandpit*. The focus on rime patterns is intended to ensure that students are not only accurate with vowel sound pronunciation but can also blend the vowels with consonant sounds that are common in syllable chunks.

Rime Patterns for Game Plan

-ish	-atch	-oth
-ick	-and	-um

Suffixes for Game Plan

-s	-es

Step 3: Teach and Review Suffixes

WINNING STRATEGY:
Spelling Rules for Words with Suffix -s and -es

Both suffix –s and –es are included in the text *The Sandpit*, and providing students with guidance on the similarities, differences, and spelling rules for using these suffixes is essential.

Determining when to use –s or –es as a suffix is dependent on the final sounds in the base word. As a reminder, both suffixes -s and -es can change the meaning of a base word in two ways. First, they can make singular nouns plural nouns (e.g. cat/cats; match/matches). Second, verbs are transformed into present tense for a singular subject (e.g. flip/He flips; fish/She fishes).

Introduction to Strategy

Teacher: *Today we will talk about the two suffixes that can make a word plural.*

Review the Job of Suffix -s

Replicate the table below that identifies the two jobs of suffix -s and examples.

Teacher: *We have already learned that suffix -s has two jobs. The first job is that it makes a noun plural.*

Teacher: *The second job of suffix -s is to create a present tense verb for a sentence about a single subject (other than you or I).*

-s	
Makes a noun plural	**Creates a present tense verb for a sentence about a single subject**
dog**s** snack**s** bell**s**	He jump**s**. The frog hop**s**.

Describe the Job of Suffix -es

Teacher: *Suffix -es performs the same job as suffix -s. Suffix -es also makes a noun plural.*

Teacher: *The second job of suffix -es is to create a present tense verb for a sentence about a single subject (other than you or I).*

-s	-es
Makes a noun plural	
dog**s**	patch**es**
snack**s**	wish**es**
bell**s**	matchbox**es**

-s	-es
Creates a present tense verb for a sentence about a single subject	
He jump**s**.	She push**es**.
The frog hop**s**.	The cat hiss**es**.

Determine When to Use Suffix -es

Teacher: *When we add the suffix -es, it gives our base word an additional syllable. Let's practice by saying the base word in isolation and then saying it with the suffix -es. (Model the chin drop method to count syllables as you pronounce each word.) Say the word "patch" with me—how many syllables? (Elicit "one.") Now say "patches." How many syllables? (Elicit "two.")*

The suffix -es is adding a syllable. (Practice with "push/pushes"; "hiss/hisses.")

Teacher: *It's important to have an extra syllable because some base words end with letters that make a "hissing sound." For example, "push," "wish," "box," and "hiss." It is hard to hear the suffix -s when the base word already hisses. So, we add a suffix with an extra syllable.*

Final Rule

Teacher: *So, our rule is when we hear a base word that ends with a hissing sound, we will add suffix -es. Final letters that make a hissing sound are 's,' 'x,' 'z,' 'sh,' or 'ch.'*

Rule for Using -es

Use -es when the base word ends with "hissing" letters.

s (glas**s**es)

x (fo**x**es)

z (buz**z**es)

sh (di**sh**es)

ch (cat**ch**es)

Step 4: Apply Phonics Concept to Single Words from the Text

The keywords in your lesson are featured in the story. They likely make an appearance in the sentence activities and will serve as a platform for practicing target phonics and morphology skills. The current Game Plan features four words from the text *The Sandpit*. Each word is relevant to the target reading skill—decoding multisyllabic words.

Individual Words for Game Plan

dishcloth

picnic

drumstick

sandwich

WINNING STRATEGY:
Backward Decoding
Multisyllabic Short Vowel Words

Some students are able to divide syllables but are challenged by accurate word reading. In certain cases, students may struggle to read individual syllables. Others might sound out each syllable correctly but inaccurately pronounce the whole word. This is when backward decoding is helpful. Instruct students to divide the syllables for each word and backward decode as necessary.

Teacher Script for Backward Decoding Multisyllabic Words from the Text

Introduction to Strategy

Teacher: *Let's continue breaking up our words by syllable. Then, I want to show you a secret strategy that helps our brain read longer words.*

Type of Words

Two-Syllable Words with Closed Syllables

Syllable Division

Write the first word: "dishcloth."

Teacher: *First, I will find the letters making vowel sounds and put dots underneath.* (Run finger under the word. Put dots under 'i' and 'o.') *We have found two vowel sounds* (indicate dots), *so we know this is a two-syllable word.*

Teacher: *The dot also indicates where our rime pattern begins. Let's underline our rime patterns.* (Underline the following patterns: d**ish**cl**oth**.) *Now we are ready to divide our word into individual syllables. We will divide after our rime patterns.* (Divide as follows: d**ish**·cl**oth**.)

Backward Decoding

Teacher: *Let's read the word from the back to the front. That way, we'll warm up our brain for words that have a similar ending pattern.* (Cover all but the last rime pattern.)

Teacher: *"-oth."* (Uncover the remaining starter consonant blend "cl.") *"cloth." The final syllable in the word is "cloth," so now our brain is activating all the words we know* that have "cloth" at the end. But we aren't going to guess. We will still read the first syllable. (Uncover the rime pattern in the first syllable and blend with the final syllable.)

Teacher: *"-ish·cloth."* (Uncover the initial sound in the first syllable and blend with remaining parts of the word.) *"dish·cloth." What is the whole word?* (Elicit "dishcloth.")

Step 5: Build Knowledge of Heart Words

Heart Words for Game Plan

island   have   give   says

Two-Syllable Heart Words

The **Teacher Script for Modeling and Practicing Reading and Writing Heart Words** is introduced in Chapter 2 (pages 52–53). Spelling two-syllable heart words is slightly different because students need to divide the word into syllables before segmenting each sound. For example, the heart word "island" is segmented into syllables using an auditory syllabification strategy such as "chin drop," where the hand is placed underneath the chin and you count each time the chin drops while pronouncing a word. The number of times the chin drops corresponds to the number of syllables in the word (e.g. is·land). Then, each syllable is segmented into individual sounds, the letters representing each sound are discussed, and the irregular spelling is highlighted using the same method as a single-syllable word. Repeat the procedure for additional words using the same prompts. As a teacher, be sure to model breaking the words into sounds and matching letters for each sound. The part of the word that is highlighted is "irregular" and has to be memorized by heart.

Chin Drop Strategy for Oral Syllable Division

The chin drop strategy is a multisensory technique that helps students count the number of syllables in a word. Students should be instructed to put their hand under their chin, palm facing down, and pronounce the word. As each vowel is pronounced, they will feel their chin drop, indicating the presence of a new syllable. Students count the number of times their chin drops to determine the number of syllables in a word.

Script for Modeling and Practicing Reading and Writing Multisyllabic Heart Words

Introduction to Strategy

Teacher: *We have been using the Heart Word Magic approach to learn how to spell and read one-syllable heart words. Now we are going to apply the same strategy to two-syllable words.*

Teacher Language and Prompt for Modeling

Teacher: *The heart word today is "island."*
Write the word on the board and use it in a sentence.
Teacher: *Say "island."*
Students repeat the word.
Teacher: *"Island" is spelled i-s-l-a-n-d.* (Spell out the word.)
Students write the word on their card.
Teacher: *"Island" is a word with more than one syllable. Let's count the number of times our chin drops when we say "island."*
Pronounce the word slowly and count the number of drops during articulation—two.

Teacher: *Two drops means two syllables. "Island" is a two-syllable word. Let's draw a slash to show there will be two syllables.*

/

Teacher: *The first syllable is /ie/—one sound (write one dash)—and is spelled 'is.' This is the tricky part of the word, and we need to memorize it by heart. So, we will place a heart underneath.*

is̲ /
♥

Teacher: *The second syllable is "land"—four sounds (/l/ /a/ /n/ /d/).*
Write three dashes.
Teacher: */l/ is spelled with 'l'*
/a/ is spelled with 'a'
/n/ is spelled with 'n'
/d/ is spelled with 'd'
All the letters are following the rules you already know, so we don't need a heart.

is̲ / l̲ a̲ n̲ d
♥

Teacher: *Let's read the heart word one more time.* (Students run their finger under the word as they read it.)
Teacher: *What was the tricky part in "island"?*
Students respond. Students add the index card to a card ring for later practice.
If students have been taught 'an' as a welded sound, adjust this script to mention three sounds in the second syllable, rather than four.

Step 6: Enhance Sight Word Recognition with RAN Charts

The Game Plan RAN charts include the individual words and phrases featured in other parts of the lesson. RAN charts are a Winning Strategy from Chapter 3 and are used to practice the automatic retrieval of common single words and phrases and support tracking across a page and the "return sweep" to the next line.

RAN Charts for Game Plan

has a dishcloth	grabs her lunchbox	Meg snatches	the drumstick
grabs her lunchbox	has a dishcloth	the drumstick	Meg snatches
Meg snatches	the drumstick	has a dishcloth	grabs her lunchbox
the drumstick	grabs her lunchbox	Meg snatches	has a dishcloth

picnic	dishcloth	sandwich	drumstick
picnic	sandwich	drumstick	dishcloth
sandwich	drumstick	dishcloth	picnic
dishcloth	picnic	drumstick	sandwich

Step 7: Practice Reading Sentences from the Text

The Game Plan has selected the following sentences from text *The Sandpit* because they include multisyllabic words (e.g. dishcloth, picnic, lunchbox, drumstick) and/or suffix -s/-es (e.g. grabs, snatches). During the Sentence Reading activity, educators can coach students to read the sentences silently, and then chorally aloud.

Sentences for Game Plan

Viv has a dishcloth with a skull on it.

"Let's have a picnic on the island," says Viv and grabs her lunchbox.

Just then, Meg snatches the drumstick!

Step 8: Expand Text-Related Vocabulary Knowledge

Activating students' knowledge of multiple-meaning words from the text supports the development of their word recognition skills. The word "drumstick" is the multiple-meaning word used in the Game Plan to deepen students' vocabulary knowledge and enhance their associations.

Vocabulary Word for Game Plan

Vocabulary Term
drumstick

Student-Friendly Definition 1
The lower part of the leg of a chicken, which is cooked and eaten. (noun)

Using the Term in a Sentence
We will have drumsticks and mashed potatoes for dinner tonight.

Student-Friendly Definition 2
Sticks used for making music on a drum. (noun)

Using the Term in a Sentence
My brother got new drumsticks in music class.

Questions for Discussion
- When might someone eat a drumstick?
- What type of musician might use drumsticks?
- How does it sound when drumsticks hit a drum?

Step 9: Putting It All Together for Text Reading and Comprehension

Building word recognition skills is a pathway to ensuring fluent reading and comprehension. Although decodable texts are short and often limited in content, the stories or texts still present opportunities to practice multiple aspects of students' comprehension, including factual, inferential, and vocabulary knowledge. The following questions on page 131 have been generated for the Game Plan.

Comprehension Questions for Game Plan

Factual
What are Fred and Viv doing in the sandpit?

Inferential
Why does Meg run off with the drumstick?

Vocabulary in Context
What does the word "bandit" mean?

Text from the Book *The Sandpit*

Viv and Fred are in the sandpit. "Let's pretend this is an island," says Viv.

Fred is a frogman. Viv has a dishcloth with a skull on it.

"Let's have a picnic on the island," says Viv and grabs her lunchbox.

Viv has a sandwich and a plum. Fred has chicken drumsticks.

"I'll give you a chicken leg for that plum." Fred hands Viv the chicken leg.

Just then, Meg snatches the drumstick! "Bandit!" yells Viv as Meg runs off.

Set a Purpose for Reading by Previewing Comprehension Questions

Educators often preview a text with students by reviewing the title, looking at the illustrations, and activating students' background knowledge about the topic. Another tool that supports setting a purpose for reading is reviewing comprehension questions for the group. By referencing the questions throughout the reading process, students are encouraged to monitor their comprehension and engage in active reading strategies.

Use Choral or Partner Reading Instead of Round Robin

Instructional approaches that support student engagement during story reading are reviewed in Chapter 1 (pages 29 and 32). The three primary engagement techniques are choral reading, partner reading, or reading to oneself. These techniques are often interchangeable. Some educators might have all students chorally read the first two pages of text and then pair off to partner read the remainder of the story. It is highly recommended that students are provided with a chance to individually "preview" the text prior to choral reading using a whisper or quiet voice. That way, they can practice or inquire about challenging words.

Step 10: Applying Phonics Knowledge to Dictation

Students benefit from a comprehensive approach that simultaneously supports the development of phonics skills for both word reading and spelling. Therefore, a selection of sounds, words, and sentences used for reading have been featured in the dictation portion of the Game Plan. Students are practicing two new spelling strategies in the current Game Plan. They are learning the rules for using suffix -es and spelling multisyllabic words for the first time.

Dictation Routine for Game Plan

Dictation	Selected Elements
Heart Word	island
Letters/Sounds/Rime Patterns	-ish, -atch, -oth
Words	dishcloth, picnic, drumstick
Sentence	Meg snatches the drumstick.

 WINNING STRATEGY:
Spelling Rules for Multisyllabic Short Vowel Words

Students often resort to guessing when spelling longer words due to limitations in phonemic awareness, phonics, or the lack of a strategic approach. As words increase in length, they typically include more complex syllable patterns, affixes, and irregular letter sequences that may be unfamiliar to

developing spellers. Research suggests that students with weaker phonological awareness may struggle to break down these complex words into manageable parts, causing them to rely on partial phonetic cues or visual approximations rather than accurate spelling rules (Treiman, 1993). As students move into spelling two-syllable words, the single most important strategy teachers provide is segmenting the word into individual syllables before attempting to spell sounds. By reinforcing segmentation strategies, teachers help the student chunk the word into parts and, similar to reading, increase their accuracy in applying phonics rules. Teachers can guide students in spelling multisyllabic words by following this procedure:

1. Model oral syllable division of spelling words using "chin drop."
2. Count the number of syllables. Draw a slash to indicate that there will be two syllables (one on each side of the slash).
3. Pronounce the first syllable.
4. Break up the first syllable into individual sounds. Draw a dash to represent each sound in the syllable, or simply represent each sound with the appropriate letters.
5. Repeat with the second syllable.
6. Guide students in checking their spelling of the word one syllable at a time.

Utilize this procedure and the script on page 133 when dictating words with two syllables for the first time. The remaining portion of the dictation routine is unchanged. Refer to Chapter 2 (pages 60–61) for the full teacher script.

Teacher Script for Introducing, Modeling, and Practicing Spelling Words with Two Syllables

Introduction to Strategy

Teacher: *All words are made up of syllables. Syllables are words or parts of words with one vowel sound. The number of vowel sounds in a word equals the number of syllables. When we spell, first say the word then count the number of syllables in the word.*

Type of Words

Two-Syllable Short Vowel Words without a Suffix

Teacher: *Your word to spell is "dishcloth."*
Students repeat the word.

Teacher: *"Dishcloth" has more than one syllable. Let's count the number of times our chin drops when we say "dishcloth." Two drops means two syllables. "Dishcloth" is a two-syllable word. Let's draw a slash to show there will be two syllables. The first syllable is "dish" with three sounds.*

$$\underline{\ \ }\ \underline{\ \ }\ \underline{\ \ }\ /$$

/d/ is spelled with 'd'
/i/ is spelled with 'i'
/sh/ is spelled with 'sh'

Teacher: *The second syllable is "cloth," which is four sounds. (Write four dashes.)*

$$\underline{d}\ \underline{i}\ \underline{sh}\ /\ \underline{\ \ }\ \underline{\ \ }\ \underline{\ \ }\ \underline{\ \ }$$

/k/ is spelled with 'c'
/l/ is spelled with 'l'
/o/ is spelled with 'o'
/th/ is spelled 'th'

Some students may need less scaffolding. For example, they may divide the word into syllables, orally segment the syllables into sounds, and then write the corresponding letter to spell the sound.

$$\underline{d}\ \underline{i}\ \underline{sh}\ /\ \underline{c}\ \underline{l}\ \underline{o}\ \underline{th}$$

Corrective Feedback

If students incorrectly write the spelling of a sound or miss a letter, use the following script.

Teacher: *What is the word you are spelling?* (Student says word.)
Have the student say the sounds and point to the letters that spell each sound. When the student points to the incorrect letter(s), use the following script.

Teacher: *You said _____. _____ is spelled _____ in the word _____.*
(Student corrects misspelling.)
Have the student say the sounds and point to the letters again to reinforce the correct spelling.

Proposed Practice Schedule

The practice schedule below suggests one method of arranging the activities into approximately 20-minute lessons over the course of three days. Please note that the first day of the lesson does not include connected text, which is a high-leverage activity for building fluency, and we recommend rereading previously learned sentences for a quick lesson warm-up.

Day 1 (18 mins)	Day 2 (23 mins)	Day 3 (20 mins)
Phonics Concept (5 mins)	Heart Words (5 mins)	RAN Chart—Phrases (5 mins)
Letter/Sound/Rime Review (3 mins)	Sentences (5 mins)	Dictation (10 mins)
Single Words (5 mins)	Vocabulary (8 mins)	Finish Book/ Read Another Book (5 mins)
RAN Chart—Single Words (5 mins)	Book Reading (5 mins)	

Game Plan

Decodable Text: *The Muffin Shop*, Dandelion Launchers Stages 16-20, Book 17b
Phonics Concept: **Reading and spelling multisyllabic words with short vowel syllables; syllable division; suffix -s/-es**

Letter/Sound/Rime Review

-est	-ess	-og	-ed
-and	-ell	-ish	-in

Phonics Concept

Provide direct instruction in the phonics concept, utilizing words pulled from the Reader and/or that fit the patterns you are teaching.

Suffix Review

-s	-es

Single Word Reading

finishes	eggshells	muffin	restless

Heart Words

says	go	into	wants

RAN Charts (Single Words and Phrases)

finishes	eggshells	muffin	restless	finishes his muffin	eggshells, hotdogs	salad, sandwiches	is restless
eggshells	finishes	restless	muffin	eggshells, hotdogs	finishes his muffin	is restless	salad, sandwiches
muffin	restless	eggshells	finishes	finishes his muffin	is restless	salad, sandwiches	eggshells, hotdogs
restless	eggshells	muffin	finishes	is restless	salad, sandwiches	eggshells, hotdogs	finishes his muffin

Sentence Reading

Fred finishes his muffin.

He is restless.

Eggshells, hotdogs, salad, sandwiches... Yuck!

Multiple-Meaning Word: tip

Definition 1 (v) To tilt or push something.	**Definition 2** (n) A suggestion or piece of advice.	**Questions** How might you react if you accidentally tip over a drink? Has anyone ever given you a tip? Did you find the tip helpful?
Sentence 1 The recipe said to tip the milk into the bowl of flour.	**Sentence 2** My art teacher gives me lots of tips about how to paint better.	

Story and Comprehension Questions

What do Fred and Mom have at the muffin shop?	Why does Fred get restless?	What makes Fred realize he put the pad and pen in the trash?

Dictation

Heart Word	wants
Letters/Sounds/Rime Patterns	-and, -ish, -est
Words	finishes, muffin, eggshells
Sentence	Fred is restless.

In practice, RAN phrases should be displayed across a single line.

Chapter 6
Spelling Strategies with Suffixes

- Rules for reading and spelling with suffix -ed

- Syntactic phrasing for sentence reading

- Rules for reading and spelling with suffix -ing

Game Plan

Decodable Text: *Stranded*, Dandelion Launchers Stages 16–20, Book 18a
Phonics Concept: Spelling multisyllabic short vowel words with -ed

Letter/Sound/Rime Review

br-	gr-	-ump
-en	-an	-unk

Phonics Concept

Provide direct instruction in the phonics concept, utilizing words pulled from the Reader and/or that fit the patterns you are teaching.

Suffix Review

-ed	-es	-s

Single Word Reading

mittens	jumped	scanned	grabbed

Heart Words

began	onto	along	tree

RAN Charts (Single Words and Phrases)

scanned	mittens	sunlit	jumped	Dennis scanned	licked his mittens	grabbed Dennis	from branch to branch
sunlit	scanned	jumped	mittens	grabbed Dennis	Dennis scanned	from branch to branch	licked his mittens
mittens	jumped	scanned	sunlit	licked his mittens	from branch to branch	Dennis scanned	grabbed Dennis
jumped	sunlit	mittens	scanned	from branch to branch	licked his mittens	grabbed Dennis	Dennis scanned

Sentence Reading

Dennis the kitten licked his mittens.

He scanned the sunlit branches.

Dennis jumped from branch to branch, up and up until he got to the top.

Multiple-Meaning Word: scan

Definition 1
(v) Looking quickly across an area to find a particular object or person.

Definition 2
(v) Using a machine to look inside like an x-ray.

Questions
Where might you need to scan a crowd or a place for a person?
What is the benefit of being able to scan something you can't see inside of?

Sentence 1
I scan the crowded auditorium, looking for my teacher.

Sentence 2
At the airport, the x-ray machines scan our bags.

Story and Comprehension Questions

Why did the branch Dennis was on crack?	Why did the robin have an advantage over Dennis the cat?	In the story, the author writes, "Dennis hatched a plan." What does it mean to hatch a plan?

Dictation

Heart Word	onto
Letters/Sounds/Rime Patterns	-an, -en, -ump
Words	mittens, jumped, grabbed
Sentence	Dennis scanned the sunlit branches.

In practice, RAN phrases should be displayed across a single line.

137

Target Skills for Game Plan

As texts become more sophisticated, sentence and word complexity increase. For example, sentences that were once simple, brief, and often formulaic (e.g. "Tam sat.") are now complex and may vary in phrase structure (e.g. "Dennis jumped from branch to branch, up and up until he got to the top."). Sophisticated sentences that contain multisyllabic words with and without suffixes require different skills for fluency and comprehension. First, ongoing effective instruction in morphology offers guidance on rules for reading and spelling suffixes. In addition, morphology instruction provides the necessary information to determine how suffixes alter the meaning of base words. Furthermore, to comprehend longer sentences and read them with intonation, students rely on syntactic knowledge to parse the text into meaningful phrases. Accordingly, there are three target skills for the current Game Plan:

- Syntactic phrasing for sentence reading
- Introducing the purpose and spelling rules for suffix -ed
- Introducing the purpose and spelling rules for suffix -ing

By providing explicit instruction that supports students' phrasing of text and spelling rules for the addition of common suffixes such as -ed and -ing, instructors support students' accuracy, automaticity, and comprehension.

Your Team

Students are ready for this lesson when they have demonstrated accuracy and fluency when reading single- and multi-syllable short vowel words, including those with beginning and ending blends. Once students have mastered these more complex rime patterns and starter sounds, they are ready for words with additional complexities, including words with suffixes beyond suffix -s and -es.

Case Study

You provide targeted Structured Literacy lessons to small groups based on instructional focus areas identified through screening data. One "at risk" student, Elijah, is a strong speller. He demonstrates solid letter-sound correspondences, but when reading aloud, you note that he sounds "staccato." When responding to comprehension questions, it is clear that Elijah has difficulty monitoring for comprehension. Another student, Nina, uses appropriate intonation when reading aloud. However, her reading is slow and labored. You are concerned that her slow pace will impact her comprehension with complex texts. When spelling, Nina demonstrates difficulty with words that are multisyllabic and include suffixes. What strategies can help Elijah and Nina develop their reading skills to move closer to benchmark reading proficiency?

Your Equipment

The Game Plan in Chapter 6 targets several different areas of skill building. The current Game Plan addresses syntactic phrasing, or the ways in which sentences are structured, along with the pronunciation and spelling rules for suffix -ed. This Game Plan is based on the text *Stranded* (Book 18a) from the **Dandelion Launchers Stages 16-20** series. Rather than using one Game Plan as a platform for practice, as was the case with previous chapters, educators will use different Game Plans provided in this chapter to support the application of different skills.

Series: Dandelion Launchers Stages 16-20
(ISBN 9781783693344)
Reader: *Stranded* (Book 18a)
Phonics Concept:
Spelling multisyllabic short vowel words; -ed with doubling.
Book Overview:
A confident cat over-estimates his hunting skills and finds himself in a tricky situation.

Text from the Book *Stranded*

Dennis the kitten licked his mittens. He scanned the sunlit branches.

Dennis spotted a robin. "I am a big cat. I can hunt," he bragged to himself.

Dennis hatched a plan. He jumped onto the tree trunk and ran along the branch.

Dennis jumped from branch to branch, up and up until he got to the top.

He inched along the thin branch. It cracked! Dennis began to swing! PANIC! HELP!

All of a sudden, a hand grabbed Dennis. "Ha! Ha! Can't get me!" chanted the robin.

Additional Texts

The additional Game Plan for Chapter 6 addresses syntactic phrasing and the spelling rules for suffix -ing (there is only one pronunciation) and is based on the text *Thinking of a Gift* (Book 19a) from **Dandelion Launchers Stages 16-20**.

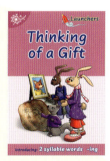

Depending on the skill level of your students, it may be necessary to provide additional opportunities for practice beyond the Game Plans in this chapter. For recommendations on texts to form the basis for crafting your own additional Game Plans, see **Additional Texts for Applying Reading and Spelling Skills for Suffix -ed** and **Additional Texts for Applying Reading and Spelling Skills for Suffix -ing** on page 140.

Additional Texts for Applying Reading and Spelling Skills for Suffix -ed

The **Dandelion Readers Set 1 Units 11-20** (Book 18) (ISBN 9780744095289), **Dandelion Readers Set 2 Units 11-20** (Book 18) (ISBN 9780744095302), and **Dandelion World Stages 16-20** (Books 18a and 18b) (ISBN 9780744095937) series target the same phonics concept as the **Dandelion Launchers Stages 16-20** (Books 18a and 18b) series, thereby providing the opportunity for instruction and application in additional texts before moving on to the next phonics concept.

Additional Texts for Applying Reading and Spelling Skills for Suffix -ing

The **Dandelion Readers Set 1 Units 11-20** (Book 19) (ISBN 9780744095289), **Dandelion Readers Set 2 Units 11-20** (Book 19) (ISBN 9780744095302), and **Dandelion World Stages 16-20** (Books 19a and 19b) (ISBN 9780744095937) series target the same phonics concept as the **Dandelion Launchers Stages 16-20** (Books 19a and 19b) series,

thereby providing the opportunity for instruction and application in additional texts before moving on to the next phonics concept.

Planning for Game Day

The Game Plan in Chapter 6 was designed using the same backward planning approach as Chapters 1–5. Backward planning ensures the activities in the Structured Literacy routines are aligned with patterns, vocabulary, and text students will encounter in the accompanying book. The sequence for backward planning is shared in the following breakout box on page 141.

Backward Planning Using a Decodable Text

Planning Reading Activities (Sentences, Single Words, RAN Charts, and Suffixes)

Step 1: Choose three sentences from the text. Select sentences that offer practice for target phonics skills.

Step 2: Select four individual words for single word reading. These words should offer practice with the target phonics skills and preferably appear in the sentences.

Step 3: Use the individual words and phrases from the sentences to create RAN charts.

Step 4: Choose suffixes to teach sound-symbol correspondence.

Planning Heart Word and Dictation Activity

Step 1: Choose up to four irregular/heart words to practice, preferably from the text.

Step 2: Plan your dictation task by selecting rime patterns, one heart word, three single words, and at least one sentence from the previous reading activities for dictation tasks.

Planning Vocabulary and Comprehension Activities

Step 1: Choose one multiple-meaning vocabulary word from the book for instruction.

Step 2: Read the text and craft questions that require students to find the information in the text (factual questions), analyze word meaning (semantic questions), or "read between the lines" to understand the deeper purpose of the story (inference questions). Set a purpose for reading by providing a question for students to keep in mind as they read the book.

Winning Strategies

The instructional routines in the Game Plan support developing students' ability to accurately read and spell words with suffixes -ed and -ing. Furthermore, the syntactic phrasing strategy supports the development of automatic phrasing and expression when reading sentences and longer passages.

- Rules for reading and spelling with suffix -ed
- Syntactic phrasing for sentence reading
- Rules for reading and spelling with suffix -ing

Rules for Reading and Spelling with Suffix -ed

Teaching the suffix -ed in an explicit and systematic manner supports understanding the purpose of the suffix, the appropriate pronunciation, and the rules related to spelling. The most straightforward aspect of suffix -ed is the way it changes the meaning of a base word. Suffix -ed is added to a verb to mean occurring in the past. The suffix is unique because it can be pronounced in three different ways, /ed/, /d/, or /t/, depending on the sounds in the base word. Furthermore, suffix -ed can impact the spelling of base words because, in some cases, it may require the addition of a second consonant letter to preserve the pronunciation of the vowel. For example, to preserve the short vowel sound /o/ in the word "hop," the consonant is doubled before -ed is added, creating the past tense of the word "hop" (hopped). If the consonant was not properly doubled, in this example the resulting word would be "hoped."

Syntactic Phrasing for Sentence Reading

Syntactic knowledge, or the understanding of sentence structure and parts of speech, is a foundational component of reading fluency and comprehension (Nation & Snowling, 2000). When children understand that words have jobs and that different words work together to create phrases, they are able to read with greater fluency and increased comprehension. For example, most English sentences follow a sequence in which verbs occur after subjects. Knowledge of typical syntactic structures helps students anticipate the flow of information, which enhances their reading fluency. In other words, understanding syntax helps students predict the relationships between words and their roles within a sentence. This offers a "roadmap" to the reader, which increases fluency. Furthermore, syntactic knowledge enhances comprehension by helping students navigate complex sentences.

Teaching parts of speech and sentence structure also equips students to decode unfamiliar words based on context. For example, in the sentence "The famished children quickly ate their entire lunch," the adjective "famished" may be unfamiliar, but the predicate phrase helps decipher the term as similar to "hungry." As a predictive skill, syntactic knowledge reduces cognitive load, enabling readers to focus on meaning rather than struggling to parse each sentence. In fact, one study that examined the relationship between syntactic knowledge of fifth grade students and their reading fluency found that children's knowledge of parts of speech enhances reading automaticity and comprehension, even when controlling for decoding ability (Mokhtari & Thompson, 2006). In the current chapter, teachers instruct students in breaking up sentences into syntactic phrases to enhance students' fluency and comprehension skills at the sentence level prior to reading the whole book.

Rules for Spelling with Suffix -ing

Although it is not as complex as suffix -ed, instruction on the spelling rules for suffix -ing provides important reading and writing support for students. When added to a base word, suffix -ing forms the present participle, or gerund, form of the verb, indicating ongoing or continuous action. The challenge with suffix -ing most often occurs during spelling. At this point, students must determine whether or not to adjust the spelling of the base word when adding the suffix. As a general rule, spelling changes occur in order to preserve the syllable type and associated vowel pronunciation of the base word. For example, when suffix -ing is added to words with two letters in the rime pattern, the reader requires a pronunciation cue to appropriately pronounce the vowel's short sound (tap + ing = tapping). That cue is the double final letter. Otherwise, readers might confuse the pronunciation of short vowel words with two-letter rime patterns and vowel-consonant-e words, particularly because when vowel-consonant-e words add suffixes, the final 'e' is dropped (tape + ing = taping). The same confusion does not occur with short vowel words with three letters in the rime pattern (e.g. stick, band, bless) because there are very few vowel-consonant-e words that have a consonant blend or digraph in the rime pattern (e.g. cache, paste). By doubling the final letter of appropriate short rime patterns, students can ensure the correct pronunciation of the vowel sound.

Rime Patterns Streamline Spelling with Suffixes

By capitalizing on students' knowledge of rime patterns, instruction in spelling rules that govern the addition of suffixes can be streamlined. For example, when determining whether the consonant needs to be doubled when adding vowel suffixes such as -ing, directing students' attention to the rime pattern can be helpful.

Students should ask themselves:
1. Does the rime pattern have a short vowel?
2. Does the rime pattern have only two letters?

If the answer to both of those questions is yes, then the final consonant should be doubled when adding a vowel suffix.

Step 1: Teach Phonics Concepts Using Winning Strategies

The phonics concepts for this chapter include reading and spelling multisyllabic words with suffix -ed and -ing. Instructions for reading multisyllabic words with -ed are presented in this section of the chapter because of the complexities involved with the task.

 WINNING STRATEGY:
Rules for Reading Words with Suffix -ed

Suffix -ed can be pronounced as three different sounds: /ed/, /d/, or /t/. The pronunciation of the suffix is complex because of the process of coarticulation, or the manner in which one speech sound is influenced by the letters that precede it. All suffixes are coarticulated with the ending of a base word.

First Sound: /ed/

When suffix -ed follows a base word that ends with either 'd' (e.g. land/landed, pad/padded) or 't,' (e.g. plant/planted, support/supported), the suffix is pronounced /ed/. This pronunciation can sometimes sound like /id/ when articulated. The pronunciation switch is related to the final 'd' and 't' in the word. These letters are paired voiced and unvoiced sounds. Paired sounds imply the two sounds share a manner and place of articulation. In the case of 'd' and 't,' the tongue is pressed against the bumpy part of the roof of the mouth behind the teeth, called the alveolar ridge. By creating a

seal between the tongue and the roof of the mouth, the sound is produced by releasing a burst of breath. When the base word ends with 'd' or 't,' the final tongue positioning makes it difficult to enunciate another similar sound (e.g. /ed/). This is the reason the vowel sound in suffix -ed can sometimes resemble /i/ rather than /e/.

Second Sound: /d/

When the base word ends with a final voiced sound other than 'd' or 't,' the /d/ sound is clearly articulated, and the additional vowel sound /e/ is not necessary. Therefore, suffix -ed makes a /d/ sound when it is coarticulated with base words that end with a voiced sound (e.g. rave/raved; club/clubbed; praise/praised).

Third Sound: /t/

When the suffix -ed is coarticulated with a base word that ends in an unvoiced sound (e.g. swish/swished; lick/licked), it is pronounced with a /t/ sound. The /t/ sound occurs in these circumstances because shifting from the pronunciation of an unvoiced sound to a /d/ sound is rather challenging. Try it with the word "bump." Force yourself to make the /d/ sound at the end of the base word—/bumpd/. You should find this difficult. In order to articulate efficiently, a shortcut results in the pronunciation of suffix -ed as /t/, which improves the overall fluency of reading and speaking these words.

Teacher Script for Introducing and Practicing the Pronunciation of the Three Sounds of Suffix -ed

Introduction to Strategy

Teacher: *Today, we will continue our discussion of suffixes. These word parts can be attached to base words and have the power to change their meaning and pronunciation.*

Type of Words

Single-Syllable Short Vowel Words with Rebellious Rime Patterns (CVCC Words)

Introduce Purpose and Pronunciation of Suffix -ed

Write "-ed" on the board.

Teacher: *Here is the suffix -ed. When suffix -ed is added to a word, it places the word in the past tense. The tricky thing is that -ed can be pronounced in three different ways. The pronunciation relies on the sounds at the end of the base word.*

Additional Words to Practice Reading

Draw a three-column table with headings that represent the three sounds of suffix -ed.

/ed/	/d/	/t/

First Sound of Suffix -ed: /ed/

Teacher: *When the base word ends with a 'd' or 't,' the suffix is pronounced /ed/. For example, let's add suffix -ed to the base word "frost": frost + ed = frosted.*

Second Sound of Suffix -ed: /d/

Teacher: *When the base word ends with a voiced final sound, the suffix makes the /d/ sound.*

For example, let's add suffix -ed to the base word "fill": fill + ed = filled.

Third Sound of Suffix -ed: /t/

Teacher: *When the base word ends with an unvoiced final sound, then the suffix makes the /t/ sound. For example, let's add the suffix -ed to the base word "pick": pick + ed = picked.*

Additional Words to Sort by Suffix -ed Sound

Have students sort additional words into the correct pronunciation column on the table you have already started.

/ed/	/d/	/t/
hunted molded	bugged jazzed	plumped brushed

The instructions for reading multisyllabic words with suffix -ing are presented in Step 3 (**Reinforce Suffix Pronunciations in Isolation**). When teaching students the three sounds of suffix -ed, it may be helpful to break up the instruction over several days. It also may be helpful to review the difference between voiced and unvoiced sounds.

Step 2: Reinforce Letters/Sounds in Isolation

The Game Plans include activities for practicing consonants, vowels, digraphs, blends, rime patterns and affixes in isolation. Teaching familiar letter patterns such as rime units, consonant blends, and affixes facilitates the recognition of word parts and enables greater automaticity in word recognition and spelling. The Game Plan features the isolated practice of two Sticky Starters and four rime patterns featured in the book *Stranded*.

Letter/Sound/Rime Review for Game Plan

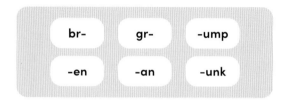

Step 3: Reinforce Suffix Pronunciations in Isolation

The current Game Plan incorporates an isolated review of previously taught suffixes. During the review, instruction elicits knowledge of suffix spelling, purpose, and varied pronunciations. In the current lesson, students will review the new suffix, -ed, as well as previously taught suffixes, -s and -es.

The suffix -ing is an important component of the additional Game Plan designed to accompany the text *Thinking of a Gift*. The suffix is introduced and practiced following the same protocols used in Chapter 4 (pages 97–99).

Suffix Review for Game Plan

Introducing Suffix –ing

Introduction to Strategy

Teacher: *We have a new suffix to learn. It is "–ing."*

Type of Suffixes

Single-Syllable Short Vowel Words with Suffix –ing

Introduce Purpose and Pronunciation of Suffix –ing

Write "–ing" on the board.

Teacher: *Here is the suffix –ing. It is spelled I-N-G and is pronounced "–ing."*

Elicit correct pronunciation.

Teacher: *When suffix –ing is added to verbs, it ensures they are in the present tense.*

Additional Practice

1. swim + ing = swimming

2. run + ing = running

3. hunt + ing = hunting

4. jump + ing = jumping

5. sob + ing = sobbing

→ Step 4: Apply Phonics Concept to Single Words from the Text

The Game Plan features four words from the text *Stranded*. Each word includes the target reading skill—decoding multisyllabic words with a suffix.

Individual Words for Game Plan

mittens jumped scanned grabbed

Practice Reading Words with Suffixes

After teaching the spelling, pronunciation, and purpose of suffixes, include activities that ensure accurate and automatic word reading.

Some students apply their knowledge of suffixes seamlessly. Others require a structured or scaffolded approach. (See the **Teacher Script for Reading Words by Base, Affix, and in Combined Form** on page 148 for a demonstration.) Although this step may be unnecessary, it becomes a helpful tool as the spelling of the base word is impacted by the presence of the suffix—for example, in words where the final letter is dropped (e.g. tape/taping) or changed (e.g. dry/dried). In these cases, a visual that depicts the base word in its original form (tape) and the compounded form (taping) reminds students that even when spellings shift, pronunciation remains the same.

Introduction to Strategy

Teacher: *Let's practice reading words with our new prefix/suffix. I will read the base word, pronounce the prefix/suffix, then combine them into the final word.*

Teacher Models	Base Word	Prefix or Suffix	Complete Word
Teacher Models	mitten	–s	mittens
Teacher and Students Together	jump	–s	jumps
Students Alone	scan	–ed	scanned
Students Alone	grab	–ed	grabbed

Providing Additional Support for Reading Multisyllabic Words with Suffixes

Some students may be able to automatically decode multisyllabic words, while others will require ongoing support. Here's a quick reminder of the steps involved.

1. Circle any suffixes and save for later reading.
2. Find and dot the letters making vowel sounds in the base word.
3. Underline the rime pattern.
4. Divide between rime patterns.
5. Backward decode the word, reading the final syllable first.
6. Blend the syllables and pronounce the whole base word.
7. Pronounce the suffix.
8. Combine the base word and suffix.

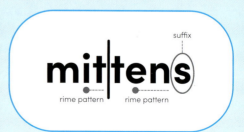

148

Step 5: Build Knowledge of Heart Words

The Game Plan has selected four heart words from the text *Stranded*. As texts become longer and more complex, heart words may increase in length. Three of the chosen heart words are two syllables (e.g. began, onto, along). The instructional strategy for teaching a two-syllable word relies on the oral segmentation of syllables using the chin drop method. See Chapter 5 (page 128) for additional information on two-syllable heart word instruction. The final heart word, "tree," is a temporarily irregular word; in other words, students may not have learned the phonics patterns yet, but they will eventually be introduced to the /ee/ sound. Educators can use their discretion about whether or not to teach a temporarily irregular word using the same protocol as for a permanently irregular word.

Heart Words for Game Plan

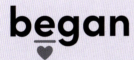

began

Syllable 1		Syllable 2		
/b/	/ee/	/g/	/a/	/n/
b	**e**	g	a	n

onto

Syllable 1		Syllable 2	
/o/	/n/	/t/	/oo/
o	n	t	**o**

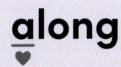

along

Syllable 1		Syllable 2	
/u/	/l/	/o/	/ng/
a	l	o	ng

tree

Syllable 1		
/t/	/r/	/ee/
t	r	**ee**

Step 6: Enhance Sight Word Recognition with RAN Charts

The Game Plan RAN charts include the individual words and phrases featured in other parts of the lesson. RAN charts are a Winning Strategy from Chapter 3 and are used to practice the automatic retrieval of common single words and phrases. They support tracking across a page and the "return sweep" to the next line.

RAN Charts for Game Plan

Dennis scanned	licked his mittens	grabbed Dennis	from branch to branch
grabbed Dennis	Dennis scanned	from branch to branch	licked his mittens
licked his mittens	from branch to branch	Dennis scanned	grabbed Dennis
from branch to branch	licked his mittens	grabbed Dennis	Dennis scanned

scanned	mittens	sunlit	jumped
sunlit	scanned	jumped	mittens
mittens	jumped	scanned	sunlit
jumped	sunlit	mittens	scanned

Step 7: Practice Reading Sentences from the Text

The current Game Plan has selected the following sentences from the text *Stranded* because they include multisyllabic words and words with suffixes.

Sentences for Game Plan

> Dennis the kitten licked his mittens.
>
> He scanned the sunlit branches.
>
> Dennis jumped from branch to branch, up and up until he got to the top.

WINNING STRATEGY: Syntactic Phrasing for Sentence Reading

A Structured Literacy framework is valuable for lesson planning because it includes instruction on multiple aspects of word knowledge. Previous chapters have focused on building abilities in phonemic awareness, phonics, semantics, and morphology. In Chapter 4 (page 96), there is a brief discussion about parts of speech to support understanding of the morphology. However, this chapter integrates robust teaching on syntax. Syntactic knowledge offers a roadmap that allows students to predict word order, support automaticity, and improve overall fluency and comprehension.

Step-by-Step Instruction for Teaching Syntactic Phrasing

Syntactic phrasing describes an approach to reading that emphasizes the structure and purpose of the sentence. In order to support students' knowledge of syntax, instruction simultaneously describes parts of speech and common phrase structures, and also supports application to sentences from the book. During the activity, teachers will visually illustrate the syntactic structure of the sentence by "scooping" words into their phrases (segmenting the phrases of the sentence with underlines). Common phrasing structures include the subject phrase, predicate/verb phrase, prepositional phrase, conjunctions, and additional clauses or objects. Students are guided to follow the scoops as they read sentences aloud. It is helpful for students to have a personal copy of the sentences for scooping and reading. This pedagogical scaffold supports the development of prosody, or intonation, and comprehension during reading.

Furthermore, in order to support students' comprehension and knowledge of syntax, teachers ask a series of comprehension questions that inquire about the different elements of the sentence. For example, "Who or what is the sentence about? What is the subject doing? When, where, or how is the action taking place?"

Common Phrases to Support Syntactic Knowledge

Subject Phrase

A subject phrase describes who/what the sentence is about. It may include more than one subject or describer word (e.g. adjectives).

Predicate or Verb Phrase

A predicate describes the action of the subject(s). A verb phrase may include description words (e.g. adverbs) or modifiers (e.g. can, has).

Conjunction

A conjunction is a word or phrase that connects two ideas (e.g. and, but, so, unless).

Prepositional Phrase

A prepositional phrase is a phrase that begins with a preposition and describes or modifies the subject, predicate noun, or verb.

Additional Clause or Object

In compound sentences, a subordinate clause further describes the predicate. An object is the person/thing that receives the effect of the predicate or subordinate clause.

Examples of phrasing structures in sample sentences:

The small pink pig	rolled	in the mud.
Subject	**Predicate**	**Preposition**

Two chipmunks, Fred and Rocket,	hunted for nuts	until	the sun set.
Preposition	**Subject**	**Predicate**	**Conjunction**

On top of the cliff,	the chicks	sat	in the nest.
Preposition	**Subject**	**Predicate**	**Preposition**

Teacher Script for Syntactic Phrasing During Sentence Reading

Introduction to Strategy

Teacher: *We are going to read some sentences. First, we will read the sentence quietly, then I will show you how to break it into phrases. Next, we will practice reading the phrases. Finally, I will ask you comprehension questions about the sentence.*

Introduce Purpose and Approach to Syntactic Phrasing

Write or project the sentence "Dennis the kitten licked his mittens."

Teacher: *First, I would like you to read the sentence quietly.*

Elicit silent reading from students.

Teacher: *Now, watch me break up the sentence into phrases.*

Scoop underneath the phrases shown below to break up the sentence. Describe the type of phrase as necessary.

Dennis the kitten	licked	his mittens.
Subject	**Predicate**	**Object**

Teacher: *Please copy the phrase scoops onto your sheet. It's your turn to read as a group.*

Students chorally read aloud, following the teacher's pointer/finger as each phrase is scooped.

Teacher: *I have a few questions to ask you about this sentence.*

Use the following prompts as appropriate:

Who is this sentence about? (Subject phrase.)

What happened to ___? (Predicate phrase.)

Where, when, or how did it happen? (Prepositional phrase.)

Did anything else happen to the subject? (For compound sentences.)

What are you picturing in your mind? (Visualization strategy.)

Repeat steps as appropriate for remaining sentences.

Additional Practice

A suggested syntactic structure for additional sentences is offered below. Sentences may be simplified or modified for this activity.

Dennis	scanned	the sunlit branches.
Subject	**Predicate**	**Object**

All of a sudden,	a hand	grabbed	Dennis.
Preposition	**Subject**	**Predicate**	**Object**

Tips for Differentiating Syntactic Phrasing

If the skills of your students vary significantly, then you may want to use some of the differentiation strategies listed below.

Modeling Fluency

Teachers begin instruction in syntactic phrasing by asking students to read the sentence quietly. Then, teachers model how to scoop the phrases in the sentence (teachers should avoid reading the sentence aloud during this step). Finally, teachers run their finger/pointer along each scoop as students chorally read the phrases aloud.

Encourage Visualization

Teachers can support the development of advanced comprehension skills by asking students what they visualize as they read each sentence, pointing students back to the text to find evidence.

Allowing Students to Create Their Own Phrases

Teachers can provide a blank copy of sentences from the text, which offers the perfect platform for advanced students to work together in pairs or individually to demonstrate their own knowledge of phrasing. It can be helpful to ask the students to familiarize themselves with the sentence by reading it before scooping it.

Connect to Tier 1/Whole Class Instruction

It might be helpful to utilize writing curriculum resources that introduce the different parts of speech in this section of the lesson plan.

Step 8: Expand Text-Related Vocabulary Knowledge

Activating students' knowledge of multiple-meaning words from the text supports the development of their word recognition skills. The word "scan" is the multiple-meaning word used in the current Game Plan to deepen students' vocabulary knowledge and enhance their associations.

Vocabulary Word for Game Plan

Vocabulary Term

scan

Student-Friendly Definition 1

Looking quickly across an area to find a particular object or person. (verb)

Using the Term in a Sentence

I scan the crowded auditorium, looking for my teacher.

Student-Friendly Definition 2

Using a machine to look inside something. (verb)

Using the Term in a Sentence

At the airport, the x-ray machines scan our bags.

Questions for Discussion

- Where might you need to scan a crowd for a person?
- What is the benefit of being able to scan something you can't see inside of?

Step 9: Putting It All Together for Text Reading and Comprehension

This activity supports both book reading and comprehension. Although the book is controlled to act as a platform for building word recognition skills with multisyllabic words with suffixes, the text also offers opportunities to engage in meaningful discussion about comprehension. The following questions have been generated for the Game Plan and the text *Stranded*. Additional strategies that enhance comprehension monitoring include activating background knowledge by previewing the title and book illustrations and setting a purpose for reading. See Chapter 1 (pages 29 and 32) for further guidance.

Comprehension Questions for Game Plan

	Text from the Book *Stranded*
Inferential Why did the branch Dennis was on crack?	Dennis the kitten licked his mittens. He scanned the sunlit branches.
	Dennis spotted a robin. "I am a big cat. I can hunt," he bragged to himself.
Inferential Why did the robin have an advantage over Dennis the cat?	Dennis hatched a plan. He jumped onto the tree trunk and ran along the branch.
	Dennis jumped from branch to branch, up and up until he got to the top.
Vocabulary in Context In the story, the author writes, "Dennis hatched a plan." What does it mean to hatch a plan?	He inched along the thin branch. It cracked! Dennis began to swing! PANIC! HELP!
	All of a sudden, a hand grabbed Dennis. "Ha! Ha! Can't get me!" chanted the robin.

Step 10: Applying Phonics Knowledge to Dictation

WINNING STRATEGY:
Spelling with Suffix -ed

Spelling words with suffixes is often complicated because writing the whole word is not simply a matter of adding the suffix. Rather, the addition of most suffixes requires a modification to the spelling of the base word. As a general rule, spelling changes occur to the base word in order to preserve the original syllable type and pronunciation of the vowel.

Students benefit from a comprehensive approach that simultaneously supports the development of phonics skills for both word reading and spelling. Therefore, a selection of sounds, words, and sentences used for reading have been featured in the dictation portion of the Game Plan. The dictation activity provides an opportunity to reinforce spelling single and multisyllabic words, as well as the strategy for spelling with suffix -ed.

Dictation Routine for Game Plan

Dictation	Selected Elements
Heart Word	onto
Letters/Sounds/ Rime Patterns	-an, -en, -ump
Words	mittens, jumped, grabbed
Sentence	Dennis scanned the sunlit branches.

Step-by-Step Instruction for Spelling with Suffix -ed

The first and most common spelling rule for adding suffix -ed is determining whether to double the final letter of the base word. One effective way for teaching this rule is to prompt students with a series of questions.

1. Does the base word have a short vowel?
2. Does the rime pattern have only two letters?

If the answer to both questions is yes, then double the final letter before adding the suffix. Practicing with spelling suffix -ed words is a productive activity that either occurs the day before the traditional dictation exercise or precedes the dictation activity.

Teacher Script to Practice Spelling with Suffix -ed					
Instruction	Teacher Models	Teacher and Students Together	Students Alone	Students Alone	Students Alone
Present base word	Let's add -ed to the word "nap."	Let's add -ed to the word "duck."	Let's add -ed to the word "stop."	Let's add -ed to the word "fill."	Let's add -ed to the word "clap."
Model "think aloud" for doubling rule	Does the base word have a short vowel? (yes) Does the rime pattern have two letters? (yes)	Does the base word have a short vowel? (yes) Does the rime pattern have two letters? (no)	Does the base word have a short vowel? (yes) Does the rime pattern have two letters? (yes)	Does the base word have a short vowel? (yes) Does the rime pattern have two letters? (no)	Does the base word have a short vowel? (yes) Does the rime pattern have two letters? (yes)
What's the doubling decision?	Yes, double the last letter— "napped."	No, do not double the last letter— "ducked."	Yes, double the last letter— "stopped."	No, do not double the last letter— "filled."	Yes, double the last letter— "clapped."

When delivering the dictation activity, educators may find the following script useful. See Chapter 5 (page 128) to review the suggested teacher language for prompting children to spell multisyllabic heart words and short vowel words.

Teacher Script for Prompted Strategy During Dictation

Teacher Prompt for Spelling Words with Suffixes

Teacher: *Your word to spell is _____.* (jumped)

Students repeat the word.

Teacher: *This is a word with the suffix -ed. Let's spell and write our base word first. Whenever we spell a word with the suffix -ed, we have to ask two questions.*

1. Does the base word have a short vowel?
2. Does the rime pattern have only two letters?

Teacher: *If the answer to both questions is yes, we double the last letter. The word "jump" has three letters in the rime pattern, so we do not double the final letter. We can just add the -ed.*

Repeat with the word "grabbed."

→ Proposed Practice Schedule

The Game Plan designed to support students at this phase of word reading development is broken into 10 steps. The plan has been broken up over the course of four days to keep sessions under 30 minutes. As always, when modifying the schedule, it is recommended that opportunities to apply skills to connected text are prioritized. It should be noted that on Days 1 and 4, connected text practice has not been identified. Teachers will want to identify appropriate texts to include on these days.

Day 1 (25 mins)		Day 2 (18 mins)		Day 3 (20 mins)	Day 4 (10 mins)
Phonics Concept (15 mins)	Suffix Review (3 mins)	RAN Chart— Single Words (3 mins)	Vocabulary (5 mins)	RAN Chart—Phrases (5 mins)	Dictation (10 mins)
				Book Reading and Comprehension (5 mins)	
Letter/Sound/ Rime Review (2 mins)	Single Words (5 mins)	Heart Words (5 mins)	Sentences (5 mins)	Practicing Spelling with Suffixes (10 mins)	

Game Plan

Letter/Sound/Rime Review

-ink	-itch	-ost
-an	-ush	-ank

Phonics Concept

Provide direct instruction in the phonics concept, utilizing words pulled from the Reader and/or that fit the patterns you are teaching.

Suffix Review

-ing	-ed	-s

Single Word Reading

stitching	getting	fixing	thinking

Heart Words

says	into	coming	are

RAN Charts (Single Words and Phrases)

stitching	fixing	thinking	getting	stitching this fabric	fixing frosted fingers	thinking of a present	getting Hank
fixing	stitching	getting	thinking	thinking of a present	stitching this fabric	getting Hank	fixing frosted fingers
thinking	getting	stitching	fixing	fixing frosted fingers	getting Hank	stitching this fabric	thinking of a present
getting	fixing	thinking	stitching	getting Hank	thinking of a present	fixing frosted fingers	stitching this fabric

Sentence Reading

"I am getting Hank a pan and a rolling pin," Alf says.

"I am stitching this fabric into a hat," says Stan.

"I am fixing frosted fingers for my pals," says Hank.

Multiple-Meaning Word: present

Definition 1 (n) Happening now.	**Definition 2** (n) A gift.	**Questions** What types of objects do we have in the present that we did not have 100 years ago? When might you receive presents?
Sentence 1 In the past, I went to bed at 7pm, but in the present I sleep at 8pm.	**Sentence 2** Amelia made a present for her mother's birthday.	

Story and Comprehension Questions

Why might Hank's pals be getting him gifts?	What do we know about Hank?	What is a synonym for "present"? What are some other meanings of the word?

Dictation

Heart Word	coming
Letters/Sounds/Rime Patterns	-ink, -itch, -ank
Words	thinking, getting, stitching
Sentence	"I am fixing frosted fingers for my pals," says Hank.

In practice, RAN phrases should be displayed across a single line.

Chapter 7

Decoding New Vowel Sounds

- Backward decoding VCe words

- Decoding multisyllabic words with short and long vowel sounds

- Spelling VCe words with suffixes using the drop 'e' rule

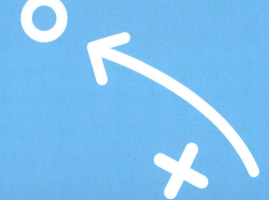

Game Plan

Letter/Sound/Rime Review

-ake	-ate	-ave
-ank	-ell	-ame

Phonics Concept

Provide direct instruction in the phonics concept, utilizing words pulled from the Reader and/or that fit the patterns you are teaching.

Suffix Review

-ed	-s	-ing

Single Word Reading

game	mates	cake	saved

Heart Words

school	said	they	goal

RAN Charts (Single Words and Phrases)

game	mates	cake	saved	lost the game	saved the day	his mates	no cake left
cake	game	saved	mates	his mates	lost the game	no cake left	lost the game
mates	saved	game	cake	saved the day	no cake left	lost the game	his mates
saved	cake	saved	game	no cake left	lost the game	his mates	saved the day

Sentence Reading

His mates lost the game.

Frank was not late for the next game.

"Frank saved the day!" his pals yelled.

Multiple-Meaning Word: game

Definition 1	Definition 2	Questions
(n) An activity or sport where you follow rules and try to win.	(adj) You are willing to try something new.	What kinds of games do people play? When playing a game, what are some things you might need? Where do people play games? What are some things that you might be game to do?
Sentence 1 Her soccer game was postponed due to bad weather.	**Sentence 2** He said he was game for a road trip to a new place.	

Story and Comprehension Questions

What seems to be a problematic pattern for Frank?	Why did Frank receive an alarm clock from Beth?	At the end of the story, Frank's pals say he "saved the day." About what other character in the story could this term be used?

Dictation

Heart Word	school
Letters/Sounds/Rime Review	-ate, -ave, -ame
Words	mates, cake, saved
Sentence	Frank's mates lost the game.

Target Skills for Game Plan

The target skills for the Game Plan focus on introducing a new syllable type—vowel-consonant-e (VCe words). The long vowels covered in the current chapter and Game Plans require a "cognitive flexing" of sorts due to the shift in vowel pronunciation. Until now, letters and their sounds have been connected through "paired associate learning," in which each letter has its "matching" sound. With the VCe syllable, students have to expand their associations to incorporate alternate sounds. The process places an additional cognitive burden on the reader. Students who demonstrated fluent word recognition with short vowel words are likely to cycle back to the Full Alphabetic/Decoding Phase when learning a new syllable type. Along these lines, there are three target skills for the current Game Plan, which lay the foundation for enhancing orthographic mapping and increasing overall reading fluency with complex texts.

- o Reading VCe words
- o Rules for spelling VCe words
- o The drop 'e' rule for spelling VCe words with suffixes/inflectional endings

Your Team

Students are ready for this type of instruction when they can accurately read single- and multi-syllable words with short vowel sounds (e.g. sun, pot, napkin, picnic). These include longer words with digraphs or blends in either the initial or final position (e.g. shin, punch, sting). Students at this phase demonstrate a basic ability to read and spell one- and two-syllable words with suffixes -s, -es, and -ing (e.g. flats, dishes, trumpets, hitting, lunchboxes). They also may have been introduced to decoding and encoding single-syllable VCe words (e.g. shine, crane, drove).

Case Study

Lee is a first grade student with solid skills reading one- and two-syllable short vowel words. Lee readily moved from the letters and sound phase to connected phonation, and then, using backward decoding, developed accuracy and automaticity with single and short vowel words. Lee regularly uses strategies such as syllable division and backward decoding to aid him in fluently reading words with two closed syllables. However, Lee reverts to sound-by-sound decoding for VCe syllable type words. What strategies can help Lee become accurate and automatic reading and spelling VCe syllable type words?

Your Equipment

Series: Dandelion Readers VCe Spellings

(ISBN 9781783693238)

Reader: *Late* (Book 1)

Phonics Concept:

Rime pattern recognition of VCe words; closed/VCe syllable division; drop 'e.'

Book Overview:

Frank's chronic tardiness causes many problems, but luckily his mom offers a great solution.

Text from the Book *Late*

Frank was late.

He was late for school.

He did not wake up.

Frank was late for Dad's birthday!

"Shame, no cake left!" said Mom.

Frank was late for the game.

His mates lost the game.

They blamed him.

Beth was upset.

"Take this!"

She gave him a box.

The box had a clock in it!

Frank was not late for the next game.

Frank saved a goal.

"Frank saved the day!" his pals yelled.

Additional Texts

As noted, the Phonic Books series simultaneously introduces the VCe syllable in single- and multi-syllable words. For some students, it may be necessary to introduce and practice single-syllable words with the VCe pattern before attempting mixed practice. In the **Dandelion Readers VCe Spellings** series, Book 1 introduces 'a-e,' pronounced with the long sound of /ae/ (also depicted as /ā/ or /A/), Book 2 introduces 'e-e,' pronounced with the long sound of /ee/ (also depicted as /ē/ or /E/), Book 3 introduces 'i-e,' pronounced with the long sound of /ie/ (also depicted as /ī/ or /I/), Book 4 introduces 'o-e,' pronounced with the long sound of /oe/ (also depicted as /ō/ or /O/), and Book 5 introduces 'u-e,' pronounced with the long sound of /ue/ (also depicted as /oo/, /ū/, or /U/). Book 6 reviews all VCe patterns. **Dandelion World VCe Spellings** (ISBN 9780593849453) is another series that follows the same progression using non-fiction texts.

Planning for Game Day

Similar to all the Game Plans in the book, this lesson was designed using a backward planning approach. By utilizing a backward planning approach, all skill development activities are aligned with patterns, vocabulary, and text that students encounter in the accompanying book. Backward planning ensures that lessons are tightly focused on building and applying a cohesive set of skills. The sequence for backward planning is shared in the following breakout box.

Backward Planning Using a Decodable Text

Planning Reading Activities (Sentences, Single Words, RAN Charts, Letter Sounds, and Suffix Review)

Step 1: Choose three sentences from the text. Select sentences that offer practice for target phonics skills.

Step 2: Select four individual words that appear in the sentences for single word reading practice.

Step 3: Use the individual words and phrases from the sentences to create your RAN charts.

Step 4: Choose starters or rime patterns to teach sound-symbol correspondence.

Step 5: Review the spelling, pronunciation, and meaning of relevant suffixes.

Planning Heart Word and Dictation Activity

Step 1: Choose up to four heart words from the text.

Step 2: Select rime patterns, one heart word, three single words, and at least one sentence from the reading activities for dictation tasks.

Planning Vocabulary and Comprehension Activities

Step 1: Choose one multiple-meaning vocabulary word from the book for instruction.

Step 2: Read the story and craft questions that require students to find the information in the text (factual questions), analyze word meaning (semantic questions), or "read between the lines" to understand the deeper purpose of the story (inference questions). Set a purpose for reading by providing a question for students to keep in mind as they read the book.

Winning Strategies

The instructional routines in the Game Plan support developing students' ability to accurately read and spell VCe words.In addition, instruction supports encoding development by teaching and practicing the rules for spelling VCe words with suffixes. The Winning Strategies in this chapter include:

- Backward decoding VCe words
- Decoding multisyllabic words with short and long vowel sounds
- Spelling VCe words with suffixes using the drop 'e' rule

Backward Decoding Single-Syllable VCe Words

Teachers can support students' efficiency in word recognition by reinforcing the use of backward decoding with single-syllable VCe words. Similar to the backward decoding instruction in Chapters 2–6, students are guided to read the rime pattern prior to the starter sound and then pronounce the whole word. This approach is especially effective for the VCe pattern because students' attention is drawn to the final silent 'e' early in the reading process. For example, the word "snake" is read "-ake," "sn-," "snake." Although counterintuitive to some who insist that words are always processed left to right, the backward decoding strategy serves several important purposes. These include breaking up the word into larger chunks, activating students' auditory memory for similar words, and supporting the accurate pronunciation of the vowel sound. Together these processes facilitate efficient orthographic mapping of the word and support the transition from decoding to sight word recognition. See Chapter 2 (page 43) for a review of the evidence supporting backward decoding.

Decoding Multisyllabic Words with Closed and VCe Syllables

When words contain multiple syllables, students require a strategic approach for systematically dividing the word into larger chunks and efficiently pronouncing each syllable. Most multisyllabic words can be decoded utilizing a few key division strategies. These approaches break up the word into small digestible units or letter patterns. Teaching and practicing syllable division methods ensures that students have a strategic approach as they encounter longer and/or unknown words. See Chapter 5 (page 117) for a review of the importance of syllable division strategies.

Spelling VCe Words with Suffixes Using the Drop 'e' Rule

Instruction on the spelling rules for adding suffixes to VCe words offers important reading and writing support for students. The process of adding suffixes to VCe words is best described by the drop 'e' rule, which requires the elimination of the final silent 'e' during the spelling process (e.g. like + ing = liking, save + ed = saved). As a reminder, no change occurs to the base word when spelling with suffix -s; writers can just add the suffix and carry on.

Step 1: Teach Phonics Concepts Using Winning Strategies

Three target phonics skills are featured in the current Game Plan. The first skill is developing accuracy and automaticity reading VCe words using the backward decoding approach. The additional phonics skills are taught during the dictation portion of the lesson.

 WINNING STRATEGY: Backward Decoding VCe Words

As described in Chapter 5, English words are composed of syllables. A syllable is a word or part of a word with one vowel sound. There are six syllable types in English. Students have already learned closed syllable words in which the vowel sound is short and closed in by a consonant. In the current Game Plan, students will practice their skills with a new syllable type, vowel-consonant-e (VCe) words. VCe words are characterized by a long vowel sound and a final silent 'e.' Practicing the pronunciation of the vowel in single-syllable VCe words offers students an opportunity to create a strong association between vowels and their new associated sounds.

Step-by-Step Instruction for Backward Decoding

The backward decoding strategy helps students process the entire word during reading, correctly pronounce the vowel sound, and move toward automatic word recognition. In order to efficiently backward decode, students must understand how to identify a rime pattern. This process is initially introduced in Chapter 2. Then, students are instructed to read the words from back to front, first reading the rime pattern, then pronouncing the starter sound in isolation, and finally blending the sounds together to produce the entire word.

Teacher Script for Backward Decoding VCe Words

Introduction to Strategy

Teacher: *Today, we are going to use our backward decoding strategy on a new syllable type. This syllable is called a vowel-consonant-e syllable because the sequence of letters in the rime pattern will be vowel, consonant, final silent 'e.' Let me demonstrate.*

Type of Word

One-Syllable Words with VCe and Closed Syllables

Syllable Division for Single-Syllable Words

Write the first word, "rake."

Teacher: *Let's find and underline the rime pattern. In order to find the rime pattern, we have to find the vowel sound and the letters that follow.*

Run finger under the word and stop at 'a.'

Teacher: *Our rime pattern is A-K-E. Notice the final silent 'e' in the word. (Point under final silent 'e.')*

Teacher: *The final silent 'e' makes the 'a' sound long—the rime pattern is "-ake." Your turn to say the rime pattern. (Elicit "-ake.")*
My turn to pronounce the starter sound—"r-." Your turn. (Elicit "r-.")
My turn to say the whole word— "rake." Your turn. (Elicit "rake.")

Additional Practice

(wake)   (same)   (plate)   (flake)

Final Silent 'e' Is Booked and Busy

In VCe words, readers rely on the presence of final silent 'e' as the primary pronunciation cue. However, final silent 'e' has several jobs in English, and they all can impact the pronunciation of the vowel. The most prominent job is influencing the vowel pronunciation so that it is a "long sound." Approximately 50 percent of words with final silent 'e' have long vowel sounds (Eide, 2012). However, it is important to let developing readers know that final silent 'e' has other jobs to do as well. See breakout box **The Many Jobs of Final Silent 'e'** on page 168. It may not be necessary to offer in-depth instruction of each of the variants of final silent 'e,' but when noticed by a student, a logical explanation can provide context for the spelling pattern.

The Many Jobs of Final Silent 'e'

Although it is most commonly associated with the pronunciation of long vowel sounds in VCe syllables, final silent 'e' serves many purposes and is one of the hardest-working letters in the English language. It is helpful to let students know that in addition to helping a vowel produce a long sound, final silent 'e' can be found doing additional jobs in other circumstances. There are nine jobs for final silent 'e' in English, and several are featured here (Eide, 2012).

Words Cannot End with 'i,' 'u,' or 'v'	As a rule, English words do not end in the three letters 'i,' 'u,' or 'v.' The placement of the final silent 'e' preserves the rule, and in some cases the vowel sound may be short (e.g. giv/give, valv/valve, solv/solve) or long (e.g. clu/clue, ti/tie). Remind students that when they hear the /j/ or /v/ sound at the end of the word, they must add a final silent 'e.'
Makes a Sound "Soft"	When final silent 'e' follows a 'c' or 'g,' the consonants are pronounced with the "soft" sounds (e.g. force, place, change, voice). Without the presence of the final 'e,' the words would be pronounced as "hard" sounds. If a word ends with a soft 'c' or 'g,' there will be a final silent 'e.'
Clarity on Pronunciation of 'th'	When digraph 'th' is followed by a final silent 'e,' the 'th' pronunciation is voiced (e.g. bath/bathe, teeth/teethe).

WINNING STRATEGY: Decoding Multisyllabic Words with Short and Long Vowel Sounds

To accurately read multisyllabic words, most students follow a set of sequential strategies. The strategy in this chapter builds on introductory instruction from Chapter 5 (page 122), in which students are taught to identify vowel sounds, underline the associated rime patterns, and divide the syllables between the rime patterns. The same practice is followed here. Once the word is accurately divided, correctly pronounce the syllables using the backward decoding method and read the last syllable first. The last step is rereading the whole word as one unit.

Teacher Script for Dividing Multisyllabic Words with VCe and Closed Syllables

Introduction to Strategy

Teacher: *Let's continue breaking up our words by syllable. You might notice two different types of syllables in these words—VCe and closed syllables. We will read our words using the backward decoding technique.*

Type of Word

Two-Syllable Words with VCe and Closed Syllables

Syllable Division for Multisyllabic Words

Write the first word, "reptile."

Teacher: *First, I am going to find the letters making vowel sounds and put dots underneath.* (Run finger under the word and put dots under the first 'e' and the 'i.')

Teacher: *We have found our two vowel sounds* (indicate dots), *so we know this is a two-syllable word. Notice that I did not put a dot under the final silent 'e' because it is not making a vowel sound. The dot also indicates where our rime pattern begins. Let's underline our rime patterns.* (Underline the following patterns: r<u>e</u>pt<u>ile</u>.)

Teacher: *Now we are ready to divide our word into individual syllables. We will divide after our rime patterns.* (Divide as follows: rep·tile.)

Teacher: *Let's backward decode the word, starting with the last syllable. Remember that this is our new syllable, VCe, so be careful of that vowel sound—"tile."* Your turn. (Elicit "tile.")

First syllable is "rep." Your turn. (Elicit "rep.")

The whole word is "reptile." Your turn. (Elicit "reptile.")

Additional Practice

pancake   sunrise   pinecone   mistake

Step 2: Reinforce Letters/Sounds in Isolation

The Game Plan features four VCe rime patterns and two closed syllable rime patterns featured in the story *Late*. The focus on rime patterns is intended to ensure that students are not only accurate with vowel sound pronunciation but can also blend the vowels with consonant sounds that are common in syllable chunks.

Letter/Sound Review for Game Plan

-ake	-ate	-ave
-ank	-ell	-ame

Step 3: Suffix Review

The Game Plan incorporates a review of previously taught suffixes. During the review, instruction elicits students' knowledge of suffix spelling, purpose, and varied pronunciations. In the current lesson, students will review previously taught suffixes –ed, –s, and –ing.

Starting in Chapter 4, suffixes are initially introduced by explicitly teaching the spelling, pronunciation, and purpose of the suffix. There are no new suffixes taught in the current chapter, but suffixes are present throughout the texts, and a review is always helpful.

Suffixes for Game Plan

-ed	-s	-ing

Step 4: Apply Phonics Concept to Single Words from the Text

The keywords in your lesson serve as a platform for practicing target phonics and morphology skills. The Game Plan features four words from the text *Late*. Each word is relevant to the target reading skill of decoding VCe words, including those with affixes.

Individual Words for Game Plan

game	mates	cake	saved

Step-by-Step Practice Reading VCe Words with Suffixes

After teaching students the pronunciation of long vowel sounds and introducing them to VCe syllables, it is helpful to include activities that ensure accurate and automatic word reading. Some students are able to apply their knowledge of VCe patterns seamlessly. Others require a structured or scaffolded approach that guides them through backward decoding the base word, pronouncing the suffix in isolation, and rereading the whole word.

A scaffolded approach is demonstrated in the **Teacher Script for Backward Decoding Words by Base, Affix, and in Combined Form**. Although this step may be unnecessary for some, it can be a helpful tool, as the spellings of many base words are impacted by the presence of a suffix. For example, in words where the final letter is dropped (e.g. tape/taped), a visual that depicts the original base word (tape) and the compounded form (taped) reminds students that even when spellings shift, pronunciation remains the same.

Teacher Script for Backward Decoding Words by Base, Affix, and in Combined Form

Introduction to Strategy

Teacher: *Let's practice reading VCe words with our new strategy. I will backward decode the base word, pronounce the suffix (if there is one), and then combine them into the complete word.*

Gradual Release Model	Base Word	Backward Decode	Suffix	Complete Word
Teacher Models	game	/ame/ + /g/ = /game/		game
Teacher and Students Together	mate	/ate/ + /m/ = /mate/	–s	mates
Students Alone	cake	/ake/ + /k/ = /cake/		cake
Students Alone	save	/ave/ + /s/ = /save/	–ed	saved

Step 5: Build Knowledge of Irregular/Heart Words

The Game Plan has four selected heart words from the text *Late*. Two of the words are permanently irregular ("said" and "they") and two of the words are temporarily irregular ("school" and "goal") because it is assumed students have not yet been taught the phonics patterns. Educators can use their discretion about whether or not to teach a temporarily irregular word using the same protocol as for a permanently irregular word. Below, these words are segmented by their sounds. The sound-symbol correspondence is presented, and any irregular spellings are noted with a heart below the letter pattern. The heart word instruction strategy is initially introduced, and a teacher script provided, in Chapter 2 (pages 51–53).

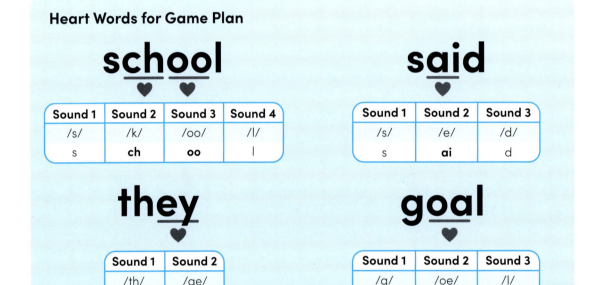

Heart Words for Game Plan

school

Sound 1	Sound 2	Sound 3	Sound 4
/s/	/k/	/oo/	/l/
s	ch	oo	l

said

Sound 1	Sound 2	Sound 3
/s/	/e/	/d/
s	ai	d

they

Sound 1	Sound 2
/th/	/ae/
th	ey

goal

Sound 1	Sound 2	Sound 3
/g/	/oe/	/l/
g	oa	l

Step 6: Enhance Sight Word Recognition with RAN Charts

Individual words and phrases from the text *Late* are used for the RAN charts. RAN charts are highlighted in Chapter 3 as a Winning Strategy and serve as a platform to practice automatic retrieval of single words and phrases. To maximize participation for all students, RAN charts should be read chorally, with students first reading the word or phrase in their head before reading as a pair or group.

RAN Charts for Game Plan

lost the game	saved the day	his mates	no cake left
his mates	lost the game	no cake left	lost the game
saved the day	no cake left	lost the game	his mates
no cake left	lost the game	his mates	saved the day

game	mates	cake	saved
cake	game	saved	mates
mates	saved	game	cake
saved	cake	saved	game

Step 7: Practice Reading Sentences from the Text

The sentence reading portion of the lesson offers students an opportunity to practice integrating decoding, heart word, and sight word skills. By selecting a variety of sentences from the decodable text as a platform for practice, students are incrementally introduced to elements of the story. This routine allows students the chance to practice backward decoding, sight word recognition, and syntactic phrasing.

Syntactic phrasing is a strategy that involves teaching students to recognize and group words into phrases based on the syntax, or structure, of sentences. This approach supports the development of both fluency and comprehension by enabling readers to process text in manageable chunks, rather than reading the sentence word by word. See Chapter 6 (page 151) for more information about syntactic phrasing. Refer to the **Teacher Script for Syntactic Phrasing During Sentence Reading** on page 175 for a demonstration of how to integrate syntactic phrasing into the lesson's sentence reading activities.

Sentences for Game Plan

His mates lost the game.

Frank was not late for the next game.

"Frank saved the day!" his pals yelled.

Punctuation Provides Clues to Prosody

Punctuation provides readers with a visual guide to written text. The use of periods and commas, as well as exclamation, question, and quotation marks, indicates where pauses, pitch changes, and intonation should occur when reading aloud. Different punctuation marks indicate varying lengths of pauses, with a comma signifying a slightly shorter pause than a period and a question mark suggesting a rising pitch at the end of a sentence. Further, punctuation also plays a role in clarifying meaning. In the famous example sentence, "Let's eat Grandma," the missing comma dramatically changes the sentence from the intended meaning that it is time to eat ("Let's eat, Grandma."). Reviewing the symbols and purpose of key punctuation is helpful for supporting students' automaticity and comprehension.

Teacher Script for Syntactic Phrasing During Sentence Reading

Introduction to Strategy

Teacher: *We are going to read some sentences. First, we are going to read the sentence quietly, then I will show you how to break it up into phrases. Next, we will practice reading the phrases. Finally, I will ask you some comprehension questions about the sentence.*

Introduce Purpose and Approach to Syntactic Phrasing

Write or project the sentence: "Frank saved the day!" his pals yelled.

Teacher: *First, I would like you to read the sentence quietly.*

Elicit silent reading from students.

Teacher: *Now, watch me break up the sentence into phrases.*

Scoop underneath the phrases shown below to break up the sentence. Describe the type of phrase as necessary.

Teacher: *Please copy the phrase scoops onto your sheet. It's your turn to read as a group.*

Students chorally read aloud, following the teacher's pointer/finger as each phrase is scooped.

Teacher: *I have a few questions to ask you about this sentence.*

Use the following prompts as appropriate:

Who is this sentence about? (Subject phrase.)

What happened to _____? (Predicate phrase.)

Where, when, or how did it happen? (Prepositional phrase.)

Did anything else happen to the subject? (For compound sentences.)

What are you picturing in your mind? (Visualization strategy.)

Repeat steps as appropriate for remaining sentences.

Additional Practice

A suggested syntactic structure for additional sentences is offered below. Sentences may be simplified or modified for this activity.

Frank's mates	lost	the game.
Subject	**Verb**	**Object**

Frank	was not late	for the next game.
Subject	**Verb Phrase**	**Prepositional Phrase**

Step 8: Expand Text-Related Vocabulary Knowledge

Activating students' knowledge of multiple-meaning words from the text supports the development of their word recognition skills. The word "game" was chosen as the multiple-meaning word for the current lesson. As in Chapters 4, 5, and 6, instruction deepens students' understanding of word meanings by providing child-friendly definitions and associations as well as illustrations of meaning.

Vocabulary Word for Game Plan

Vocabulary Term
game

Student-Friendly Definition 1
An activity or sport where you follow rules and try to win. (noun)

Using the Term in a Sentence
Her soccer game was postponed due to bad weather.

Student-Friendly Definition 2
You are willing to try something new. (adjective)

Using the Term in a Sentence
He said he was game for a road trip to a new place.

Questions for Discussion
- What kinds of games do people play?
- When playing a game, what are some things you might need?
- Where do people play games?
- What are some things that you might be game to do?

Step 9: Putting It All Together for Text Reading and Comprehension

The following questions have been generated for the current Game Plan and the text *Late*. See Chapter 1 (pages 29 and 32) for guidance on engaging strategies for reading aloud, including the use of choral reading.

Comprehension Questions for Game Plan

Factual
What is a problematic pattern for Frank?

Inferential
Why did Frank receive an alarm clock from Beth?

Vocabulary in Context
At the end of the story, Frank's pals say he "saved the day." About what other character in the story could this term be used?

Text from the Book *Late*

Frank was late.

He was late for school.

He did not wake up.

Frank was late for Dad's birthday!

"Shame, no cake left!" said Mom.

Frank was late for the game.

His mates lost the game.

They blamed him.

Beth was upset.

"Take this!"

She gave him a box.

The box had a clock in it!

Frank was not late for the next game.

Frank saved a goal.

"Frank saved the day!" his pals yelled.

Step 10: Applying Phonics Knowledge to Dictation

Students benefit from a comprehensive approach that simultaneously supports the development of phonics skills for both word reading and spelling. Therefore, a selection of sounds, words, and sentences used for reading have been featured in the dictation portion of the Game Plan. The dictation activity provides an opportunity to reinforce spelling of single-syllable VCe words and the strategy for adding suffixes to VCe words.

Dictation Routine for Game Plan

Dictation	Selected Elements
Heart Word	school
Letters/Rime Patterns	-ate, -ave, -ame
Words	mates, cake, saved
Sentence	Frank's mates lost the game.

 WINNING STRATEGY: Spelling VCe Words with Suffixes Using the Drop 'e' Rule

Similar to the suffix spelling strategies introduced in Chapter 6, it is important for students to consider the pattern of the base word before adding a suffix. As a general rule, spelling changes occur to the base word in order to preserve the original syllable type and pronunciation of the vowel. The drop 'e' rule provides students with a strategic approach for adding a suffix to single-syllable or multi-syllable words ending with final silent 'e.'

Step-by-Step Instruction for the Drop 'e' Rule

The drop 'e' rule cues the reader to pronounce the base word's vowel as a long sound. One effective way for teaching the drop 'e' rule is to prompt students with a series of questions.

1. Does the base word end in a final silent 'e'?
2. Does the suffix begin with a vowel?

If the answer to both questions is yes, drop the final silent 'e' before adding the suffix. If the answer to either question is no, do not drop the 'e' before adding the suffix. See the **Teacher Script to Practice Drop 'e'** and the **Teacher Script for Prompted Strategies During Dictation** on page 179 for suggested teacher language.

Practicing spelling VCe words with suffixes is a productive activity that should occur either the day before the traditional dictation exercise or directly precede it. When delivering this activity, it is helpful to scaffold the spelling conversation.

Teacher Script to Practice Drop 'e'

Instruction	Teacher Models	Teacher and Students Together	Students Alone	Students Alone	Students Alone
Present base word	Let's add "-ed" to the word "flake."	Let's add "-ed" to the word "cave."	Let's add "-s" to the word "plate."	Let's add "-ing" to the word "make."	Let's add "-ing" to the word "race."
Model "think aloud" for drop 'e' rule	Does the base word have a final silent 'e'? (yes) Does the suffix begin with a vowel? (yes)	Does the base word have a final silent 'e'? (yes) Does the suffix begin with a vowel? (yes)	Does the base word have a final silent 'e'? (yes) Does the suffix begin with a vowel? (no)	Does the base word have a final silent 'e'? (yes) Does the suffix begin with a vowel? (yes)	Does the base word have a final silent 'e'? (yes) Does the suffix begin with a vowel? (yes)
What is the drop 'e' rule?	Yes, drop the final silent 'e'—"flaked."	Yes, drop the final silent 'e'—"caved."	No, just add the 's' and carry on—"plates."	Yes, drop the final silent 'e'—"making."	Yes, drop the final silent 'e'—"racing."

Teacher Script for Prompted Strategies During Dictation

Spelling Words with Suffixes

Teacher: *Your word to spell is _____.*
   (saved)

Students repeat the word.

Teacher: *This is a word with the suffix -ed. Let's spell and write our base word first. For words with final silent 'e,' ask these questions:*

1. Does the base word have a final silent 'e'?
2. Does the suffix begin with a vowel?

Teacher: *If the answer to both questions is yes, drop the 'e' before adding the suffix.*

Teacher: *The word to spell is _____.*
   (mates)

Students repeat the word.

Teacher: *This is a word with the suffix -s. Let's spell and write our base word first. For words with final silent 'e,' ask these questions:*

1. Does the base word have a final silent 'e'?
2. Does the suffix begin with a vowel?

Teacher: *If both answers are yes, drop the 'e.' If the answer to one question is no, do not drop the 'e.'*

Proposed Practice Schedule

The Game Plan for this phase of word reading is broken into 10 steps. The plan has been broken up over the course of four days to keep sessions to 20 minutes or under. As always, when modifying the schedule, it is recommended that opportunities to apply skills to connected text are prioritized. Connected text practice has not been identified on Days 1 and 4. Teachers will want to identify appropriate texts to include on these days.

Day 1 (20 mins)		Day 2 (18 mins)		Day 3 (20 mins)	Day 4 (10 mins)
Phonics Concept (10 mins)	Suffix Review (3 mins)	RAN Chart—Single Words (3 mins)	Vocabulary (5 mins)	RAN Chart—Phrases (5 mins)	Dictation (10 mins)
				Book Reading and Comprehension Questions (5 mins)	
Letter Sounds for Rime Patterns (2 mins)	Single Words (5 mins)	Heart Words (5 mins)	Sentences (5 mins)	Introduce and Practice with Drop 'e' (10 mins)	

Game Plan

Letter/Sound/Rime Review

-ete	-ese	-ask
-ess	-ash	-ish

Phonics Concept

Provide direct instruction in the phonics concept, utilizing words pulled from the Reader and/or that fit the patterns you are teaching.

Suffix Review

-ed	-es	-s

Single Word Reading

completed	delete	concrete	these

Heart Words

began	is	to	said

RAN Charts (Single Words and Phrases)

completed	delete	concrete	these	completed his task	on the concrete	pressed delete	these dishes
delete	completed	these	concrete	pressed delete	completed his task	these dishes	on the concrete
concrete	these	completed	delete	on the concrete	these dishes	completed his task	pressed delete
these	delete	concrete	completed	these dishes	pressed delete	on the concrete	completed his task

Sentence Reading

That evening, Dad completed his task.

The glass smashed on the concrete.

Dad had to stop him and pressed 'delete'!

Multiple-Meaning Word: concrete

Definition 1
(n) A liquid substance used for building that hardens quickly.

Definition 2
(adj) Something that is specific and real.

Questions
What does it mean to have concrete plans?
What are some things that concrete is used to build?

Sentence 1
The truck arrived to pour the concrete for the house's foundation.

Sentence 2
We need concrete evidence that you are working on the project.

Story and Comprehension Questions

What happens when Pete tries to help Mom?

How did Mom feel in the end?

Why does the author write "snapped Mom," instead of "said Mom"?

Dictation

Heart Word	began
Letters/Sounds/Rime Patterns	-ete, -ask, -ish
Words	complete, these, delete
Sentence	The glass smashed on the concrete.

In practice, RAN phrases should be displayed across a single line.

Glossary

Auditory memory The ability to take in, process, store, and recall orally presented information

Automaticity The ability to effortlessly read words without having to decode them

Backward decoding Decoding a syllable by the rime unit before the onset (e.g. reading "-ake," then "fl-," then saying "flake")

Backward planning A strategic approach to instruction that involves starting with the desired outcome and working backward to identify the steps or skills needed to reach the goal

Choral reading A technique where all students in the group (or class) read in unison in order to optimize opportunities for practice

Consolidated Alphabetic Phase One of Linnea Ehri's phases of word reading where students develop the ability to automatically pronounce entire words without decoding

Consonant A speech sound that is produced by obstructing the airflow in the vocal tract

Consonant digraph Two consonants that work together to represent a single sound (phoneme) (e.g. sh, th, ch, etc.)

Context processor The part of the brain that uses surrounding information to confirm meaning (Four-Part Processing Model)

Continuous blending An instructional technique for sounding out words without pausing between sounds (sometimes called connected phonation)

Continuous sound A sound (phoneme) that can be elongated without becoming distorted; all vowels are continuous sounds, as well as some consonants, including 's' and 'm'

Decodable text Highly controlled reading material that aligns with phonics skills students have been taught, allowing students to decode, or sound out, words to practice skills in connected text

Decoding The process of using letter-sound knowledge to blend sounds together to read words

Dictation A teaching technique where teachers say sounds, words, or sentences aloud and students demonstrate knowledge by writing the appropriate sound, word, or sentence

Encoding Using knowledge of sounds (phonemes) to spell words

Explicit instruction A structured, teacher-led approach involving step-by-step directions, demonstration, and plentiful practice opportunities

Fluency A reading behavior that indicates a reader is automatic across all aspects of word knowledge; characterized by prosodic and effortless reading so energy can be dedicated to understanding content/meaning

Four-Part Processing Model A model of how the brain learns to read, highlighting the interactive nature of multiple aspects of language knowledge, including phonological, orthographic, semantic, and context in reading development

Full Alphabetic Phase One of Linnea Ehri's phases of word reading where students attend to every letter in a word and have an understanding of the sound-symbol relationship in order to convert letters into sounds and blend to pronounce words

Heart word High-frequency words that contain one or more irregular spelling patterns

High-frequency word The most commonly occurring words in text (e.g. the, of, and); high-frequency words may be considered irregular words or heart words

Letter-sound correspondence The relationship between letters and their corresponding sounds (also known as sound-symbol or grapheme-phoneme correspondence)

Meaning processor The part of the brain that connects words to their meanings (Four-Part Processing Model)

Morpheme The smallest unit of meaning

Morphology The study of meaningful word parts (morphemes) and how they combine to form words

Onset The part of a syllable that precedes the vowel; onsets consist of one or more consonants

Orthographic mapping The mental process by which readers store written words and their spellings to long-term memory for instant recognition, enabling fluent reading

Orthographic processor The part of the brain that focuses on the visual patterns of letters and their combinations, allowing for identification of letters and words (Four-Part Processing Model)

Partial Alphabetic Phase One of Linnea Ehri's phases of word reading where students are just beginning to make letter-sound connections

Phonemic awareness The ability to hear, identify, and manipulate individual sounds in words

Phonological awareness The ability to understand, recognize, and manipulate spoken language, including words, syllables, onsets/rimes, and phonemes; an essential early reading skill

Phonological processor The part of the brain responsible for recognizing, processing, and manipulating sounds in spoken language (Four-Part Processing Model)

Pre-Alphabetic Phase The first phase in Linnea Ehri's phases of word reading where children rely on visual cues, rather than letter-sound relationships, to recognize words

Prosody The rhythm, stress, and intonation patterns in a spoken language that contribute to overall understanding

RAN chart Rapid Automatic Naming chart; a tool that provides a repeated presentation of single words or phrases from a text, offering the automatic retrieval of common single words and phrases

Reading circuit The network in the brain that allows for the connection of visual and linguistic processes

Rebellious rime patterns Closed syllables where the vowel makes the long sound rather than the expected short sound (sometimes called closed syllable exception words)

Rime pattern The part of a syllable that includes the vowel and any letters after it

Scarborough's Reading Rope A model illustrating the complex and interconnected skills involved in proficient reading; the reading rope depicts two intertwined strands, word recognition and language comprehension, which are both critical to developing fluent and meaningful reading

Science of Reading A body of research that draws on the fields of neuroscience, cognitive science, and linguistics that identifies the most effective reading instruction methods based on how people learn to read

Scooping Grouping words in phrases

Segmenting Breaking words apart into individual phonemes; segmenting is a key part of phonemic awareness and is integral to the ability to decode and spell words

Semantic neighborhood A group of words that have similar meanings or are connected in some way

Semantics The study of the meaning of words, phrases, and sentences

Sight word Any words that are recognized and read automatically, meaning that they do not need to be sounded out, or decoded

Simple View of Reading A theory positing that reading comprehension is the result of two factors: decoding and language comprehension; weakness in one component will impact overall reading comprehension

Simultaneous Oral Spelling A multisensory method of teaching spelling that uses visual, auditory, and kinesthetic learning to spell words

Sound-symbol correspondence See Letter-sound correspondence

Starter sound The first part of a word or syllable that appears before the rime (e.g. /b/ in "bat," /sh/ in "ship"); the initial sound

Stop sound A consonant sound that is made by briefly blocking airflow and releasing it (e.g. /b/, /p/, /k/, /t/)

Structured Literacy An evidenced-based approach to teaching reading and spelling that provides explicit, systematic, cumulative, and diagnostic instruction to develop foundational literacy skills

Suffix A word part added to the end of a base word that changes its meaning or grammatical function

Syllable A word or part of a word with one vowel sound

Syntactic phrasing Grouping words into meaningful phrases while reading in order to support understanding

Syntax The set of rules that governs how words, phrases, and clauses are arranged to form clear and meaningful sentences

Unvoiced sounds Speech sounds that are produced without the vibration of vocal cords (e.g. /f/, /k/, /p/, /t/, /s/)

Visual word form area Also known as the brain's "letterbox," this area of the brain is specialized for recognition of letters, letter strings, and words and interacts with other language-related areas of the brain as part of the reading circuit

Voiced sounds Speech sounds that are produced with the vibration of the vocal cords (e.g. /b/, /d/, /g/, /v/, /z/)

Vowel A speech sound produced without blocking the airflow

Welded sounds Groups of letters where individual sounds are closely connected and potentially altered due to articulation, making them difficult to separate (e.g. an, am, all, ank, ing) (also referred to as glued sounds)

Index

Acknowledgments

R. C. Anderson et al, *Becoming a nation of readers: The report of the Commission on Reading*, National Institute of Education, 1985. (page 15)

J. M. Anglin, G. A. Miller, and P. C. Wakefield, "Vocabulary development: A morphological analysis," *Monographs of the Society for Research in Child Development*, 58 (10), 1993. (pages 91, 117)

A. L. Archer and C. A. Hughes, *Explicit Instruction: Effective and Efficient Teaching*, Guilford Press, 2011. (pages 7, 29, 36, 62)

I. L. Beck, M. G. McKeown, and L. Kucan, *Bringing Words to Life: Robust Vocabulary Instruction*, Guilford Press, 2013. (pages 12, 83, 106)

C. F. A. Benjamin and N. Gaab, "What's the story? The tale of reading fluency told at speed," *Human Brain Mapping*, 33 (11), 2012. (page 9)

B. A. Blachman et al, *Road to the Code: A Phonological Awareness Program for Young Children*, Brookes Publishing Co., 2000. (page 33)

L. Buchanan, C. Burgess, and K. Lund, "Overcrowding in semantic neighborhoods: Modeling deep dyslexia," *Brain and Cognition*, 32 (2), 1996. (pages 12, 81)

S. J. Carrier, "Effective strategies for teaching science vocabulary," LEARN North Carolina: UNC-Chapel Hill, NC, 2011. (page 92)

S . Dehaene, *Reading in the Brain: The New Science of How We Read*, Penguin, 2010. (page 9)

G. Di Pietro, "The impact of Covid-19 on student achievement: Evidence from a recent meta-analysis," *Educational Research Review*, 39, 2023. (page 6)

R. E. Donegan and J. Wanzek, "Effects of reading interventions implemented for upper elementary struggling readers: A look at recent research," *Reading and Writing*, 34 (8), 2021. (pages 7–8)

N. K. Duke et al, "Authentic literacy activities for developing comprehension and writing," *The Reading Teacher*, 60 (4), 2006. (page 15)

L. C. Ehri, "Learning to read words: Theory, findings, and issues," *Scientific Studies of Reading*, 9 (2), 2005. (page 30)

L. C. Ehri, "Orthographic Mapping in the Acquisition of Sight Word Reading, Spelling Memory, and Vocabulary Learning," *Scientific Studies of Reading*, 18 (1), 2014.

L. C. Ehri, "Phases of development in learning to read words by sight," *Journal of Research in Reading*, 18 (2), 1995. (page 9)

D. Eide, *Uncovering the Logic of English: A Common-Sense Approach to Reading, Spelling, and Literacy*, Pedia Learning Inc., 2012. (pages 118, 167–168)

J. M. Fletcher et al, *Learning Disabilities: From Identification to Intervention*, Guilford Press, 2018. (page 7)

B. Foorman et al, "Foundational Skills to Support Reading for Understanding in Kindergarten through 3rd Grade." (NCEE 2016-4008), Washington, DC: National Center for Education Evaluation and Regional Assistance, Institute of Education Sciences, U.S. Department of Education, 2016. Available at: http://whatworks.ed.gov (page 7)

K. Galuschka et al, "Effectiveness of spelling interventions for learners with dyslexia: A meta-analysis and systematic review," *Educational Psychologist*, 55 (1), 2020. (page 44)

R. Gersten et al, "Assisting students struggling with reading: Response to Intervention and multi-tier intervention for reading in the primary grades. A practice guide" (NCEE 2009-4045), Washington, DC: National Center for Education Evaluation and Regional Assistance, Institute of Education Sciences, US Department of Education, 2008. Available at: https://ies.ed.gov/ncee/wwc/practiceguides (page 15)

R. Gersten et al, "Meta-analysis of the impact of reading interventions for students in the primary grades," *Journal of Research on Educational Effectiveness*, 13 (2), 2020. (page 7)

S. M. Gonzalez-Frey and L. C. Ehri, "Connected phonation is more effective than segmented phonation for teaching beginning readers to decode unfamiliar words," *Scientific Studies of Reading*, 25 (3), 2021. (page 23)

P. B. Gough and W. E. Tunmer, "Decoding, reading, and reading disability," *RASE: Remedial and Special Education*, 7 (1), 1986. (pages 8, 30, 54)

S. Graham, "The sciences of reading and writing must become more fully integrated," *Reading Research Quarterly*, 55 (S1), 2020. (page 84)

S. Graham and T. Santangelo, "Does spelling instruction make students better spellers, readers, and writers? A meta-analytic review," *Reading and Writing*, 27 (9), 2014. (page 44)

S. Graham, K. R. Harris, and B. F. Chorzempa, "Contribution of spelling instruction to the spelling, writing, and reading of poor spellers," *Journal of Educational Psychology*, 94 (4), 2002. (page 58)

J. Hasbrouck and R. Parker, "Quick phonics screener," St Paul, MN: Read Naturally, 2006. (page 67)

A. K. Hudson et al, "Elementary teachers' knowledge of foundational literacy skills: A critical piece of the puzzle in the science of reading," *Reading Research Quarterly*, 56 (S1), 2021. (page 6)

D. A. Kilpatrick, *Essentials of Assessing, Preventing, and Overcoming Reading Difficulties*, John Wiley & Sons, 2015. (page 43)

D. A. Kilpatrick, *Equipped for Reading Success: A Comprehensive, Step-by-Step Program for Developing Phoneme Awareness and Fluent Word Recognition*, Casey & Kirsch Publishers, 2020. (pages 10–11, 44, 46, 102, 117)

M. R. Kuhn, "What's Really Wrong with Round Robin Reading?," International Literacy Association, *Literacy Now*, 2014. Available at: https://www.literacyworldwide.org/blog/literacy-now/2014/05/07/what%27s-really-wrong-with-round-robin-reading- (page 33)

J. B. Lindsey, *Reading Above the Fray: Reliable, Research-Based Routines for Developing Decoding Skills*, Scholastic, 2022. (page 15)

M. W. Lovett et al, "Development and evaluation of a research-based intervention program for children and adolescents with reading disabilities," *Perspectives on Language and Literacy*, 40 (3), 2014. (pages 7–8)

B. D. McCandliss, L. Cohen, and S. Dehaene, "The visual word form area: expertise for reading in the fusiform gyrus," *Trends in Cognitive Sciences*, 7 (7), 2003. (page 20)

D. Mewhort and A. Beal, "Mechanisms of word identification," *Journal of Experimental Psychology: Human Perception and Performance*, 3 (4), 1977. (page 118)

L. C. Moats, "Teaching reading is rocket science: What expert teachers of reading should know and be able to do," *American Educator*, 44 (2), 2020. (pages 6, 58)

L. C. Moats and S. Brady, *Speech to Print: Language essentials for Teachers*, Paul H. Brookes Publishing Company, 2000. (pages 23, 33)

K. C. Moats and C. Tolman, "Module 3: Spellography for Teachers: How English Spelling Works", excerpted from *Language Essentials for Teachers of Reading and Spelling (LETRS)*, Boston: Sopris West, 2009. (page 58)

K. Mokhtari and H. B. Thompson, "How problems of reading fluency and comprehension are related to difficulties in syntactic awareness skills among fifth graders," *Literacy Research and Instruction*, 46 (1), 2006. (page 142)

R. D. Morris et al, "Multiple-component remediation for developmental reading disabilities: IQ, socioeconomic status, and race as factors in remedial outcome," *Journal of Learning Disabilities*, 45 (2), 2012. (pages 7–8)

K. Nation and M. J. Snowling, "Factors influencing syntactic awareness skills in normal readers and poor comprehenders," *Applied Psycholinguistics*, 21 (2), 2000. (page 142)

National Reading Panel (US), "Teaching children to read: An evidence-based assessment of the scientific research literature on reading and its implications for reading instruction," National Institute of Child Health and Human Development, 2000. (pages 7, 9, 24, 30, 32, 43)

M. Orkin et al, "The more you know: How teaching multiple aspects of word knowledge builds fluency skills," *The Reading League Journal*, 3 (2), 2022. (page 4)

C. Perfetti, "Reading ability: Lexical quality to comprehension," *Scientific Studies of Reading*, 11 (4), 2007. (page 30)

P. M. Pexman et al, "There are many ways to be rich: Effects of three measures of semantic richness on visual word recognition," *Psychonomic Bulletin & Review*, 15, 2008. (pages 71, 105, 108)

P. M. Pexman, S. J. Lupker, and Y. Hino, "The impact of feedback semantics in visual word recognition: Number-of-features effects in lexical decision and naming tasks," *Psychonomic Bulletin & Review*, 9 (3), 2002. (page 12)

Reading Rockets, "Books for practicing letter-sound relationships," Reading Rockets, 2024. Available at: https://www.readingrockets.org/classroom/choosing-and-using-classroom-texts/using-decodable-books (page 15)

Really Great Reading, "Beginning and Advanced Decoding Surveys," Cabin John, MD: Really Great Reading Company, 2010. (page 67)

Really Great Reading, "Heart Word Magic," Cabin John, MD: Really Great Reading Company, 2024. Available at: https://www.reallygreatreading.com/resources/heart-word-magic (page 44)

D. M. Rehfeld et al, "A meta-analysis of phonemic awareness instruction provided to children suspected of having a reading disability," *Language, Speech, and Hearing Services in Schools*, 53 (4), 2022. (page 24)

H. S. Scarborough, "Connecting early language and literacy to later reading (dis) abilities: Evidence, theory, and practice," in S. Neuman and D. Dickinson, *Handbook for Research in Early Literacy*, Guilford Press, 1, 2001. (pages 8, 54)

M. S. Seidenberg and J. L. McClelland, "A distributed, developmental model of word recognition and naming," *Psychological Review*, 96 (4), 1989. (pages 8, 70)

L. Spear-Swerling, *The Structured Literacy Planner: Designing Interventions for Common Reading Difficulties, Grades 1–9*, Guilford Publications, 2024. (page 15)

M. L. Stanback, "Syllable and rime patterns for teaching reading: Analysis of a frequency-based vocabulary of 17,602 words," *Annals of Dyslexia*, 42, 1992. (pages 13, 119–120)

K. E. Stanovich, R. G. Nathan, and M. Vala-Rossi, "Developmental changes in the cognitive correlates of reading ability and the developmental lag hypothesis," *Reading Research Quarterly*, 21 (3), 1986. (page 15)

R. Treiman, *Beginning to Spell: A Study of First-Grade Children*, Oxford University Press, 1993. (page 132)

W. E. Tunmer and J. W. Chapman, "The simple view of reading redux: Vocabulary knowledge and the independent components hypothesis," *Journal of Learning Disabilities*, 45 (5), 2012. (page 15)

J. Wanzek et al, "Current evidence on the effects of intensive early reading interventions," *Journal of Learning Disabilities*, 51 (6), 2018. (page 7)

M. Wolf, *Proust and the Squid: The Story and Science of the Reading Brain*, HarperCollins, 2007. (page 7)

M. Wolf, "RAVE-O Instructor Manual Volumes 1 & 2," Frederick, CO: Cambium Learning Group, 2011. (page 8)

M. Wolf, "The Reading Brain: The Canary in the Mind." *Emerging Trends in the Social and Behavioral Sciences: An Interdisciplinary, Searchable, and Linkable Resource*, 2017. (page 9)

M. Wolf et al, "The RAVE-O intervention: Connecting neuroscience to the classroom," *Mind, Brain, and Education*, 3 (2), 2009. (pages 78, 104)

M. Wolf and M. B. Denckla, *RAN/RAS: Rapid Automatized Naming and Rapid Alternating Stimulus Tests*, Austin, TX: Pro-ed, 2005. (page 78)

M. Wolf and T. Katzir-Cohen, "Reading fluency and its intervention," *Scientific Studies of Reading*, 5 (3), 2001. (pages 4, 9, 70)

T. S. Wright and G. N. Cervetti, "A systematic review of the research on vocabulary instruction that impacts text comprehension," *Reading Research Quarterly*, 52 (2), 2017. (pages 92, 107)

M. J. Yap et al, "An abundance of riches: Cross-task comparisons of semantic richness effects in visual word recognition," *Frontiers in Human Neuroscience*, 6, 2012. (page 81)

G. K Zipf, "The meaning-frequency relationship of words," *Journal of General Psychology*, 33, 1945. (page 92)

M. Zipke, L. C. Ehri, and H. S. Cairns, "Using semantic ambiguity instruction to improve third graders' metalinguistic awareness and reading comprehension: An experimental study," *Reading Research Quarterly*, 44 (3), 2009. (page 92)

Picture Credits

The publisher would like to thank the following for their kind permission to reproduce their photographs:
(Key: a-above; b-below/bottom; c-center; f-far; l-left; r-right; t-top)

Sarah Gannon: 191cr; **Alexandria Osburn:** Tim Cameron 191br; **Shutterstock.com:** AboutLife - Raev Denis 155cra, Jaromir Chalabala 106tr, DGLimages 75, fast-stock 58, Ground Picture 106cr, Grustock 130crb, Yuganov Konstantin 123, MBLifestyle 130cra, Monkey Business Images 80, Kostikova Natalia 81, Okrasiuk 82tr, Orion Production 155cr, PeopleImages.com - Yuri A 26, 76, 93, 100, 140, 166, PHkorsart 82, pics five 176, Alessandro Pintus 40, Rido 18, Studio Romantic 104, Sunny studio 176br

About the Authors

Melissa Orkin is an educator and developmental psychologist who specializes in literacy achievement. Melissa has served as a researcher and instructor at Tufts University. As the director of the educational consulting group Crafting Minds, Melissa collaborates with educators across New England and lives with her family in the Boston area.

Sarah Gannon is a former third grade teacher, reading specialist, literacy coach, and Orton-Gillingham practitioner. In her current role as co-director of Crafting Minds, Sarah translates educational research into practical strategies and curriculum resources for teachers. She resides outside of Boston with her husband and three children.

Alexandria Osburn has enjoyed her career as a special educator, reading specialist, literacy coach, and Wilson® Dyslexia Practitioner. She is passionate about translating research to practice and creating educator-friendly Structured Literacy resources. Alex lives on Lake Winnipesaukee with her loving husband.

Professional Learning Community Discussion Guide

This guide is designed to support educators in exploring effective literacy instruction strategies and applying them in their classrooms. Each section includes discussion points to encourage collaboration, reflection, and actionable steps that give educators the opportunity to exchange insights, address challenges, and develop strategies tailored to the unique needs of their learners.

Initial Thoughts	• Which phase of word recognition best aligns with your current small group's reading skills? • Why is it important to integrate often neglected elements of early literacy instruction, including vocabulary, syntax, and comprehension? • How might integrating a multi-componential approach represent a shift from current practices?
Chapter 1	• Consider the case of Cameron. How might each Winning Strategy from the chapter support her in moving to the next phase of word reading development? • Which Winning Strategies would you like to integrate into your instruction? • How does backward planning support a cohesive lesson plan? • How might backward planning maximize instructional time and student achievement?
Chapter 2	• Consider the case of Matteo. How might each Winning Strategy support him in moving to the next phase of word reading development? • How does an approach that emphasizes rime patterns support word recognition skills? • For many educators, the Heart Word approach represents a shift from current "trick word" instruction. What benefits might this approach represent? • Choose 1–2 heart words from a decodable text. Take turns utilizing the script to introduce the Heart Word Magic strategy to your colleagues.
Chapter 3	• Consider the case of Sienna. How might each Winning Strategy support Sienna in moving to the next phase of word reading development? • What considerations need to be made when delivering RAN chart instruction to ensure that all students are engaged?
Chapter 4	• Consider the case of Jonah. How might each Winning Strategy support Jonah in building stamina with longer words? • What are the benefits of focusing vocabulary instruction on multiple-meaning words? Choose a decodable text and identify multiple-meaning words that lend themselves to this type of instruction.
Chapter 5	• Consider the case of Geoff. How might each Winning Strategy support him in decoding multisyllabic words? • How can teaching single-syllable words utilizing a rime pattern approach support accuracy and fluency when reading multisyllabic words? • Consider your experience instructing students in syllable types and/or syllable division. What strategies worked well? What challenges have you encountered while teaching this?
Chapter 6	• Consider the cases of Elijah and Nina. How might each Winning Strategy support Elijah and Nina's ability to spell with suffixes? • How does instruction in syntactic knowledge support a multi-componential approach to reading? How might sentence-level comprehension questions support fluency and comprehension?
Chapter 7	• Consider the case of Lee. How might each Winning Strategy support Lee in building sight word recognition with new vowel sounds? • What is both complex and essential about teaching suffixes?
Final Thoughts	• Consider how the template for the Structured Literacy plan has evolved from Chapter 1 to Chapter 5. Make note of strategies that are introduced or faded. How do these adaptations support students at various phases of word recognition? How are each of the POSSUM components reinforced? • Choose a decodable book for one of your small groups. Identify the appropriate phase of word reading development. Backward plan a lesson appropriate for that phase.